# the manager's
# COMMUNICATION
# Toolbox

Everett Chasen and Bob Putnam

**ASTD Press** is an internationally renowned source of insightful and practical information on workplace learning and performance topics, including training basics, evaluation and return-on-investment, instructional systems development, e-learning, leadership, and career development.

**Ordering information:** Books published by ASTD Press can be purchased by visiting ASTD's website at store.astd.org or by calling 800.628.2783 or 703.683.8100.

Library of Congress Control Number: 2012948621
ISBN-10: 1-56286-818-7
ISBN-13: 978-1-56286-818-5

**ASTD Press Editorial Staff:**

Director: Glenn Saltzman
Manager, ASTD Press: Ashley McDonald
Associate Editor: Heidi Smith
Community of Practice Manager, Workforce Development: Ron Lippock
Proofreader: Stephanie Castellano
Editorial Assistant: Sarah Cough
Design and Production: Marisa Kelly
Cover Design: Ana Foreman

Printed by: Versa Press, East Peoria, IL,
www.versapress.com

# TABLE OF CONTENTS

# INTRODUCTION

When baseball scouts travel the world looking for young players who might become the all-stars of tomorrow, they evaluate their subjects in five categories: hitting for average, hitting for power, speed, fielding ability, and throwing ability. A player with outstanding ability in each of the five areas is called a "five-tool player."

In the business world, above-average employees with leadership potential must be competent in five basic communication skills. Every leader, from the president of the United States to the assembly-line supervisor at an automobile plant, must be able to read, write, speak, think, and listen at advanced levels. By mastering these five communication skills, managers enhance their interaction with employees and business contacts to form a positive and productive environment for success.

"Five-tool" managers—those who read quickly, critically, and comprehensively; who write with speed and clarity; who present their ideas in an understandable manner; who are always one or two steps ahead in their thought processes; and who listen actively and empathetically—are highly prized and sought-after. Occasionally, such a person will be identified while toiling away at a nonsupervisory job. But the odds of finding such a diamond in the rough are nearly the same as visiting a sandlot baseball field in Alabama and spotting the next Willie Mays.

It's much more likely that managers who read, write, speak, listen, and think well will stand out from their peers, and will be closely watched by top management. Want to be one of those stars? Then you need the same thing all baseball players with the potential for greatness need: good coaching and training.

If you're looking for improvement in one, two, or even all five of these crucial communication skill areas, *The Manager's Communication Toolbox* is the place to start. Within these pages, we offer simple and effective tactics to help managers improve their ability to communicate with staff, peers, supervisors, and the public.

Our book can be read from cover to cover—or in sections, depending on what you need. There is no shortage of books, courses, and training materials covering each of the areas we discuss, but we also know a manager (especially if she's new) has little time to read an entire book when confronting a deadline. Accordingly, we've kept our chapters well-defined, and packed each one with as much essential information and helpful hints as possible. We hope our book will serve as a touchstone for you throughout your career—one you'll always keep close at hand.

Have you ever been asked to give an important speech or presentation? We'll tell you how to stay calm and under control, how to use visual aids, and how to prepare. Are you overwhelmed by the volume of information you're expected to master for your job? We'll explain how to skim documents, how to prioritize emails, and how to successfully manage an inbox. We'll offer you tips on how to run a meeting: how to forge consensus; how to listen well and give feedback; and how to be both a leader and a team player at the same time.

Our book includes expert tips from several leaders who credit their success, in large part, to effective communication. Our list of interviewees includes a former cabinet secretary; one of the nation's leading trial lawyers; the presidents of two major trade associations; a retired U.S. Army general who subsequently led the nation's largest healthcare organization; several senior human resource professionals for large corporations, and many others. Their insights will illuminate your path to career success.

We'll also share our own experiences as communicators with you. Both of us have founded and run successful communication companies, providing counseling and writing services to dozens of satisfied clients. We've each been professional speechwriters; for more than two decades, our words have helped clients get their points across effectively. Bob is in considerable demand as a speaker, and as an instructor on public speaking and other communication techniques. Ev is a recently retired member of the federal Senior Executive Service, where he has successfully managed a large number of employees.

Together, we have more than 70 years of experience and stories to share. We know we can turn employees with minor league communication skills into major league talents. Let's play ball!

# READ QUICKLY AND EFFICIENTLY

"Books serve to show a man that those original
thoughts of his aren't very new after all."

— *Abraham Lincoln*

---

### In This Chapter

- Enrich your vocabulary and improve comprehension.
- Skim a publication quickly.
- Understand a writer's message by taking notes.
- Absorb the most in the least amount of time.
- Adjust your reading rates to fit the material.

---

Reading is a fundamental—perhaps the most fundamental—communication skill. No manager can perform well on any job without the ability to read well and carefully. Every manager has to read reports, answer emails, and interpret memos to act upon them. Without good reading skills, it is difficult for a manager to absorb all the information needed for success, and it will end up taking longer for a manager to react in changing situations.

Reading is vital to developing the mind. It enhances vocabulary, and enables managers to communicate with precision—so they can have and show more intelligence and authority. Reading well-written books improves your writing skills because you are observing and appreciating the craft of writing. Reading improves your thinking and speaking skills by showing you ways to express yourself more clearly and with flair. Plus, your listening skills improve as you learn to focus on what a writer communicates.

Besides improving the other four skills discussed in this book—thinking, writing, speaking, and listening—reading is a great source of new ideas. It's also a superb way to understand other people and their points of view, a critical skill every successful manager must develop. Reading creates respect; it demonstrates you are an educated and thoughtful person, which are keys to being well regarded.

Every manager reads. Those who read widely and well have a competitive edge, are more creative, and think more clearly than those who limit their reading to work-related matters. In this chapter, we'll help you improve your ability to read a book, article, website, or other document—not for pleasure, but to gain and retain knowledge.

**EXPERT TIP**

**Robert Kole, PhD,** is a retired professor of composition and literature at the City University of New York and the Polytechnic Institute of New York. To improve your reading comprehension, Professor Kole suggests:

- **Reading without remembering is of little value.** When you read a book, you should underline it, write about it, talk about it, and think about it. "I keep talking about what I've read. That's the way I remember what's important."

- **Reading for business requires concentration.** Sit at a desk and read with a notebook or legal pad right next to you. "Just the act of writing things down will help you retain what you've read."

- **Write your thoughts in a notebook, instead of underlining in the book.** A notebook makes it easier to keep track of your insights. "If I write too much in a book, it becomes very hard to reread."

- **Reading is integral to professional advancement.** "The impressive person is the person who has read more thoroughly than everyone else. You become the 'go-to' person in your organization and your profession."

## How to Read a Book

Mortimer Adler and Charles Van Doren wrote *How to Read a Book*. Perhaps the book's greatest contribution is its fifth chapter, "How to Be a Demanding Reader." In it, they offer suggestions for how to write notes in a book.

Writing in a book is "an expression of your differences or agreements with the author. It is the highest compliment you can pay him (Adler and Van Doren, 1972)." Using a book's margins or underlining important passages are not just ways to remember what you've read. These tips remind you to take action when you've read something of value.

Adler and Van Doren suggest the following system of marking a book.

- Underline major points and forceful statements.
- Draw vertical lines at the margin to emphasize underlined points, or to highlight areas too long to be underlined.
- Use stars, asterisks, or other doodads in the margin to highlight the most important points in the book (not more than ten).
- Use numbers in the margin to sequence arguments the author makes in support of his point.

- Circle important or memorable phrases.
- Write on the sides, top, or bottom of the pages to ask questions; simplify complex statements in your own words; and record how major points progress through the book.

You can also use the blank pages at the front of most books to summarize the text and its most important points. Plus, you can also create an electronic file with brief summaries of everything you've read.

Too much writing in a book will make it unreadable. And if you're reading a library book, of course, you can't mark the text—so keep an electronic or print journal handy, and jot down page numbers of significant passages so you can find what you're looking for again.

Marking a book or keeping a pad by your side while reading helps you remember by emphasizing what *you* think is useful—not what the author thinks will be helpful. Taking notes helps you review the book later, and keeps you focused on the book instead of on distractions.

If you can, read in a comfortable spot. That's probably not your office. It may be your organization's library, a park bench in an office complex, the local coffee shop, or your desk at home. Stop reading if you get tired, and take time to think about what the author is saying. But don't put a book aside for extended periods, or you'll lose its thread. Also, some people can read and listen to music, but people usually can't read and watch television at the same time. They won't retain the book's content.

When you've completed the book, evaluate it. Think about whether the author's evidence supports the book's conclusions—and whether they have proven those conclusions. Go a little further: Are the conclusions always true in all cases? Are the opposite of the conclusions false? And, most importantly, are they true for you based on your own experience? That kind of critical thinking is essential for analyzing any book.

## Improve Your Vocabulary

Developing a strong vocabulary is essential for a manager. It improves your reading speed and comprehension because you stop stumbling over unfamiliar words. It will also help you communicate to your staff and others with accuracy and precision. Just like every other skill in this chapter, the best way to improve your vocabulary is to read more.

When you speak with others, especially around the workplace, listen for unfamiliar words. These words will probably relate to your profession. At the first convenient moment, jot them down, look them up in a dictionary, and use them. (You shouldn't interrupt conversations to jot down unfamiliar words, though. Wait a few minutes until no one's around before doing so.)

Keep a small pad handy to write down unfamiliar words you come across during the day, or enter them into your phone or other personal assistant device. If you write in the margins of a book or in your journal and you looked up a word in the dictionary, write a brief definition of the word, or a synonym for it in your book or journal. Then you'll remember what you've learned.

There are several free online dictionaries—put the link to one in the "Favorites" section of your Internet browser. Make sure you have a dictionary on your office bookshelf, and another at home. Keep your home dictionary near your favorite reading spot. If you've got to get up and go to another room to use it, you probably won't! E-books offer an advantage here: Most have built-in dictionaries so you can look up words just by pointing to them.

There are lots of vocabulary-building software programs and books available, along with word-a-day software and calendars. The goal of learning a new word every day is a good one. If you buy a vocabulary book for this purpose, make sure you get one that's not too hard or too easy for you. You can also try opening a dictionary to a random page and finding an unfamiliar word to learn. Playing games like Scrabble® or Words With Friends® will also help. A good place to start any word-a-day effort is with words that pertain to your business, or one of your hobbies. And if you use the new words you've learned as quickly as possible, you'll find you remember them better!

---

**Reminder 1.1**
Most words have common roots, prefixes, and suffixes.

| **prefix** = at the beginning of a word that changes the word's meaning. | **root** = the foundation on which its basic meaning is built. | **suffix** = at the end of a word that changes the word's meaning. |
|---|---|---|

*Example:* untenable = not able to hold on

| **prefix** un=not | **root** ten=holding | **suffix** able=able to |
|---|---|---|

---

You can often determine a word's meaning from the way it is used in a sentence. You may not know, for example, what the word "hearsay" means in a court of law. But read the sentence: "Because Mary did not actually see the accident take place, the judge dismissed her testimony as hearsay." You can then determine that hearsay is evidence produced by a witness who did not see or hear the incident but heard about it from someone else. You also learn that hearsay is generally not admissible as evidence in a trial.

## Read to Fit the Material

Speed-reading is a good idea for some books and documents, but some books are critically important to your job performance or are densely written, so they need to be digested and studied. You might, for example, read the latest *Twilight* novel or something by Tom Clancy quickly, but you need to read a book like Malcolm Gladwell's *Outliers* more slowly.

For nonfiction works, use the table of contents—the book's outline—as a guide to which parts of the book can be read completely, and which can be skimmed, or whether the book is worth your time at all. After checking out the table of contents, read—don't skim—the introduction. Introductions give you a sense of the author's writing style. If you can't make it through the introduction without getting bored, that's a good hint you'll have problems with the rest of the book. More importantly, the introduction will tell you why the author wrote the book and which subjects she will address.

If the author's message could help you solve a problem or improve your managerial skills, read on. If you can't figure out the author's message from the introduction, or if it doesn't look like the book is going to meet your needs, find something else to read! Life's too short, and there are too many alternatives. The same applies to magazine articles, journals, and blog posts. We'll talk more about selecting the right things to read in chapter 2.

If you don't need detail, skim chapters in the book that don't directly pertain to what you want from it. Here is the best way to skim: Read the first sentence of every paragraph and then choose full paragraphs that help you get information you want. Always read chapter introductions and summaries, though, and pay attention to diagrams, charts, and other inserts.

## Improve Speed

Twenty or 30 years ago, speed-reading was all the rage. Many courses promised to improve your reading speed and comprehension, freeing you to do other things with the time you saved. Some of these courses and books still exist today, but so many people had disappointing results that these classes are no longer as popular. While there are no shortcuts, there are some tips you can use to improve your reading speed.

The best way to improve your reading speed is, quite simply, to read more often. The more you read, the more your vocabulary will improve and the less you'll stumble over unfamiliar words. You can also practice reading more quickly, training your eyes to take in more words with every glance.

If you move your lips when you read, train yourself to stop. And if you hear every word in your head as you read, try to stop that habit, too. Hearing words in your head is called subvocalization. You should be able to read far more quickly than you can speak, and moving your lips limits you to reading at a speaking speed. One way to eliminate subvocalization is to chew gum or hum while reading. That keeps your vocal cords busy!

Many people listen to music when they read, but if your goal is to read more quickly, do so without a soundtrack. Other distractions, like the ping of your email inbox, or your colleagues sticking their heads in your door, should also be avoided if possible. If you pay attention to what you read the first time, you'll minimize the number of paragraphs you have to reread for comprehension.

Using a pencil, pen, or your finger can improve your speed. Don't move it across the page word by word, but rather down the page, line by line. The faster you move it, the faster your eye will follow, and the faster you'll read. Try it first with a document you've already read and see how quickly you can go. Then try it with documents you haven't read, but are familiar with. Finally, use the technique with unfamiliar documents that are hard to read.

Use your peripheral vision; you don't constantly move your head from left to right when you're driving, so try reading down the middle of the page and catching the words on the sides of the page. Again, this technique takes practice: Start with something you're familiar with and work your way up to more difficult text. Draw a line down the center of the page and concentrate on that.

As you practice reading faster, check that your ability to comprehend what you've read hasn't suffered. There's no sense improving your speed if you no longer understand what you've read. You'll simply have to reread the material, and no time will be saved.

## Analyze the Material

Once you've read the book, Adler and Van Doren suggest you answer the following questions.

- What is the book about as a whole?
- What is being said in detail and how?
- Is the book true, in whole or in part?
- What is the significance of the work?

They also suggest you write a short paragraph describing what the book is about. Consider sharing the paragraph with others: Post it to a website that accepts book reviews, such as Amazon.com. Writing for others helps clarify your thoughts and opinions, and it will help others decide whether the book you've read will also help them. Of course, you should also use other people's reviews as a guide to your own reading!

# WHAT TO READ

"Outside of a dog, a book is man's best friend. Inside of
a dog, it's too dark to read."

—*Groucho Marx*

---

### In This Chapter

- Why read business material?
- Five business books to read.
- Five magazines to read.
- Five podcasts to listen to.
- Hints on how to choose materials that improve
  managerial ability, solve real-life problems, and give
  the big picture about your profession, industry, and
  career path.

---

According to Jack Covert and Phil Sattersten, authors of *The 100 Best Business Books of All Time*, 11,000 business books were published in a recent year in the United States alone (Covert and Sattersten, 2009). No one can read even a fraction of that number, especially while earning a living at the same time.

Managers have other important things to read besides the latest business books. Business magazines, blogs, and podcasts also compete for readers' limited attention—as do the emails, memorandums, reports, and other materials that pile up on their desks every day. When you consider the enormity of the task of keeping up with everything that's out there, it's awfully tempting to just chuck whatever you're reading in favor of a *Seinfeld* rerun or the latest Brad Pitt movie.

Reading for business, however, is an extremely valuable use of your time. As Covert and Sattersten point out, business books are "a high-value proposition for 20 dollars and two hours of your attention." They help you do your jobs better; they explain how other people and companies—including many of the world's most successful managers and organizations—have responded to the same challenges you face; and they offer the best thoughts of professors who study the practice of management.

Reading is a conversation between the writer and the reader. In fact, it's the best kind of conversation—the kind in which one party (the writer) has carefully thought about what to say before saying it. Because of this, the reader has the advantage of receiving the writer's best thoughts without the digressions, omissions, and unsupported assertions that frustrate even the most useful face-to-face discussions.

**EXPERT TIP**

The author of five business-related books, **Stewart Liff** reads widely in other genres as well. He chooses books largely through recommendations from friends and people he likes and respects—and by browsing the business sections of bookstores. Liff's own career as an author, consultant, teacher, public speaker, and artist owes much to having read biographies, "for the opportunity to see how great leaders face and overcome challenges in their own lives."

**Reminder 2.1**

Where to Buy

*Bookstore:* advantage of knowledgeable staff to provide personal recommendations.

*Internet:* some sites have personalization to provide general recommendations and customer reviews.

How to Choose

- Read the back of the book and inside cover flap.
- Read the introduction.
- Consider the content and the writing style.

## Five Books to Read

A large number of books about business, management, and leadership were read to prepare this book. Because of the wide variety of business books, it's hard to say anyone is qualified to assess all of them. It is a tough job for anyone, anywhere, to compile an essential list for managers consisting of only five books.

In 2011, *Time* magazine chose the 100 best nonfiction books written since 1923, which was the year *Time* began publishing. They included business classics such as *How to Win Friends and Influence People* by Dale Carnegie, a book still widely read 75 years after it was first published. It also included Richard N. Bolles' *What Color Is Your Parachute?* which was self-published in 1970, and its wisdom has guided job seekers ever since.

---

**Figure 2.1**

Time Magazine's All-Time Best Business Books

- *Capitalism and Freedom*, by Milton Friedman (published in 1962)
- *Fast Food Nation*, by Bryan Walsh (published in 2001)
- *The General Theory of Employment, Interest, and Money*, by John Maynard Keynes (published in 1936)
- *How to Win Friends and Influence People*, by Dale Carnegie (published in 1937)
- *No Logo*, by Naomi Klein (published in 2000)
- *Unsafe at Any Speed*, by Ralph Nader (published in 1965)
- *What Color Is Your Parachute?*, by Richard Nelson Bolles (published in 1970)

---

As noted above, Covert and Sattersten also choose 100 books for their personal list. Others have named 20, 25, and 99 books—but it's tough to name just five. Here are the ones we've chosen that offer practical advice you need in just a few pages.

**The Elements of Style, by William Strunk, Jr. and E.B. White.** Will Strunk was a professor of English at Cornell University. He wrote *The Elements of Style* in 1918 as a manual to help Cornell students and faculty write more clearly. One of Professor Strunk's students was E.B. "Andy" White. White, the author of *Charlotte's Web* and *Stuart Little* and a long-time contributor to *The New Yorker*, revised the book for republication. The revised manual is on *Time's* list of 100 best nonfiction books. Now in its fourth edition, the book offers 11 elementary rules of English usage; 11 elementary principles of composition; and 21 hints on how to develop your own writing style (our favorites are numbers 14, "Avoid fancy words," and 16, "Be clear"). The book is not written for those who choose writing as a profession, but for everyone else who must write occasionally, including students and business people. In the foreword to the book's current edition, Roger Angell succinctly states: "Writing is hard." Reading *The Elements of Style* makes it easier.

**Coping With Difficult People, by Robert M. Bramson, PhD.** Nothing is more difficult or gut-wrenching than dealing with a subordinate who seems determined to be a pain. Bramson explains—by personality type—how some people approach making you miserable, and how to neutralize their behavior. The book is easy to read, easy to refer to (it's a good idea to reread chapters just before possible confrontational meetings), and doesn't attempt to change difficult employees. Instead, Bramson offers hundreds of useful suggestions to change your own behavior so you can deal effectively with problem employees.

**In Search of Excellence: Lessons From America's Best-Run Companies, by Thomas J. Peters and Robert H. Waterman.** Many of the companies cited as examples of excellence are no longer among America's best run, such as Digital Equipment Corporation, an early computer manufacturer. The principles of corporate success that Peters and Waterman identified, however, are still valid.

These are all concepts that still apply to well-managed organizations today: having a bias for action; staying close to the customer; encouraging autonomy and entrepreneurship; putting people first; hands-on, value-driven management; sticking with the business the company knows best; keeping organizations simple and lean; fostering a climate where everyone knows and understands the company's values; and allowing employees to flourish within those values.

***Strictly Speaking*, by Reid Buckley.** Some readers may remember William F. Buckley, Jr.—an author, television commentator, columnist, and one of the founders of the modern conservative movement. His brother Reid founded the Buckley School of Public Speaking in 1988. While not as prolific an author as his late brother, Reid Buckley has given us perhaps the best book on public speaking for professionals. The book includes six chapters on the mechanics of being a good speaker; 10 cardinal sins amateurs commit (number two: never begin a speech with a joke) and 10 commandments all speakers must observe (number six: be not only succinct, be brief.) If you find you need more information on how to speak like a manager, this is the book you should have.

***Rules and Tools for Leaders*, by Perry M. Smith.** General Smith's intended audience is not new managers, but those about to assume command of larger organizations. Most of his insights, however, are extremely valuable to managers on any level. His chapter on hiring the right people for the right jobs includes a list of questions to ask applicants that are perfect for conducting a successful interview. His recommendation that leaders should look for opportunities to demonstrate their integrity early on in their tenure is one of the finest pieces of advice any new manager could receive. Lots of checklists on how to hire, fire, plan, deal with the media, and other subjects make this book remarkably helpful to managers at all stages of their careers.

## Five Magazines to Read

In the era of the Internet, print media are declining in number and in circulation. Many websites such as *The Huffington Post*, *The Daily Beast*, and *Grantland* provide the kind of content that once would have been found only in print form. They can be considered the 21st-century version of the magazine format. But whether you read your magazines in print form, online, or on a tablet, these publications, like books, offer great value and insight for your money.

Magazines keep you abreast of what's going on in your business, your community, and the world. Keep in mind that if you don't know of a new development, you won't be able to find out about it through a search engine, but you will learn of it in the pages of a magazine! Good magazines, like great books, offer you the best thinking about business on a regular basis. Unlike books, however, magazines are able to offer advice that's extremely timely. While books take years to write and publish, magazines take only days or weeks—and those with online versions cut that brief timeline even more.

Virtually every industry—including government—offers many trade-specific magazines. Make sure you know which publications cover your industry, and subscribe to them (often, those subscriptions are free). Five general business magazines we think every manager should read regularly include:

**Bloomberg Businessweek**—a weekly magazine offering in-depth news and analysis on global business, finance, and the world economy, plus expert opinions on major companies, industries, policies, and technology.

**Forbes**—the magazine famous for its list of the "400 Richest People in America," and for other lists, including "America's Best Small Companies" and the "World's Most Powerful People."

**Fast Company**—a 10-issue-per-year magazine geared toward younger businesspeople and entrepreneurs.

**Fortune**—the longtime biweekly competitor to *Forbes* and *Bloomberg Businessweek*, known for its researched and ranked lists—especially the Fortune 500, which ranks companies by their gross revenues.

**Harvard Business Review**—a 10-issue-per-year magazine, which offers the latest research on managerial excellence (subscribers get access to HBR's online archive, an invaluable bonus).

## Five Blogs to Follow

Newspapers and magazines are declining, but blogging is ascending. Blogs are online journals, available only on the Internet, in which people, companies, and even news publications share their thoughts, knowledge, and expertise.

A number of the best thinkers and writers on the subjects of leadership and management write blogs, and many of them are worth following. To choose which blogs to follow, look for ones that teach you things about leadership you don't already know. Second, look for bloggers who can write clearly and well—many, alas, cannot. Third, look for bloggers who are passionate about their subjects. And finally, look for bloggers who have no biases, other than toward the truth as they understand it.

While there are many blogs on leadership worth reading, here are five to check out (most of them, as is blogger custom, include a list of blogs they also follow). If you like what they're writing, you will probably like what they're interested in as well.

**Leadership Freak (www.leadershipfreak.wordpress.com)**—The subtitle of Dan Rockwell's blog is "Helping Leaders Reach Higher in 300 Words or Less," and he regularly delivers pithy essays on leadership that contain more insight than many 300-page books.

**Tompeters! (www.tompeters.com)**—Tom Peters, the coauthor of *In Search of Excellence*, (recommended in our book section) and his company have an outstanding management blog. Besides management posts, Peters and company include videos, slide presentations, podcasts, and other useful information. Peters calls his blog posts "dispatches from the new world of work."

**Great Leadership (www.greatleadershipbydan.com)**—Dan McCarthy is the director of executive development programs at the Whittemore School of Business and Economics at the University of New Hampshire. His thoughtful, detailed blog posts offer useful guidance to leaders from new supervisors to CEOs.

*Ask a Manager* (www.askamanager.com)—For the perspective of a female manager, try Allison Green's *Ask a Manager* blog. She often explains to nonmanagers why managers do what they do—a particularly useful perspective for new managers.

*The Bing Blog* (stanleybing.blogs.fortune.cnn.com.)—Stanley Bing, author of nine books on business and who also writes for *Fortune*, may be the funniest business writer working today. His offbeat observations will simultaneously entertain and inform you. His blog is a great read!

One caveat: blogs are ephemeral. Many are here today, abandoned tomorrow. We believe the ones we've chosen have staying power—but, caveat emptor (let the buyer beware)!

## Five Podcasts to Listen to

Podcasts are audio files found on the Internet that you can transfer to your iPod or to any device that plays MP3s. Individuals who want to share their knowledge on a particular subject create podcasts. Many businesses offer podcasts to reach out to their customers and others. Websites such as *Podcast Alley* (www.podcastalley.com) categorize and review podcasts.

Podcasts are easy to listen to on your commute, and offer much information and opinions on leadership. Here are five podcasts on leadership and management to check out:

*HBR IdeaCast*—The publishers of *Harvard Business Review* magazine create a new podcast every week with what they describe as "breakthrough ideas and commentary from the leading thinkers in business and management." All of their podcasts are free, and are available from Apple's iTunes store.

*London Business School*—The London Business School also makes podcasts on business and leadership available on iTunes. Many are from professors at the school, and some are from business leaders with a slightly different perspective—from across the pond.

*What Great Bosses Know*—The Poynter Institute is a school dedicated to teaching and inspiring journalists and media leaders. They hope to encourage the kind of journalism that informs citizens and enlightens public discourse. Jill Geisler, the Institute's leadership and management expert, produces this series of podcasts to "help anyone who hopes to be a great boss, or to work for one."

*CEO Exchange*—The Public Broadcasting System's website (www.pbs.org) offers a compilation of the audio tracks of *CEO Exchange*, an hour-long television program featuring interesting and innovative CEOs from throughout the world. The program's host, noted journalist Jeff Greenfield, focuses on the human side of the CEO, not the business side—and the interviews he conducts provide remarkable insights on leadership and career development.

**Center for Creative Leadership**—The Center for Creative Leadership is an organization that has focused on leadership education and research since 1970. Their definition of creative leadership is giving leaders capacity to achieve more than people imagine by enabling them to think and act beyond boundaries. Their extensive library of podcasts covers all aspects of leadership and management.

Of course, there are hundreds—even thousands—more useful books, magazines, blogs, and podcasts managers will benefit from reading or following. Reading widely for pleasure also helps. The sources we've listed will give you a head start on exploring each of these areas. Being a successful manager means committing yourself to a lifetime of learning and self-improvement.

**CHAPTER 3**

# WHAT IS GOOD WRITING?

"A writer is someone for whom writing is more
difficult than it is for other people."

—*Author Thomas Mann*

---

### In This Chapter

- Why you should write well.
- What a manager needs to know to write
  knowledgeably and persuasively.

---

The French Emperor Napoleon Bonaparte, who controlled nearly all of Europe for a brief time in the early 19th century, led an army made up of an estimated 600,000 men. Among them was a young corporal who has gone down in history with the unfortunate nickname of "Napoleon's Idiot." Whenever Napoleon wrote an order to his commanders or his troops, he would read it to the corporal before issuing it. Bonaparte would then ask the man to tell him, in his own words, what the Emperor had just told him. If the corporal could do so successfully, Napoleon published the order. If not, Napoleon would rewrite his order until this soldier clearly understood what the Emperor wanted his men to do.

Writing to be understood is as important for you, as a manager, as it was for Napoleon. Perhaps more so, because in that era most people were illiterate—while today, nearly everyone writes, and many write well. The Internet has returned the written word as a major communication tool.

Twitter, with its 140-character limit, has resulted in a kind of shorthand that regularly horrifies high-school grammar teachers. Yet thousands of blogs and websites demonstrate how millions of Americans can write well, in both the content and comment sections. They effectively persuade, inform, share experiences and emotions, and communicate with audiences both known and unknown. Most people who regularly post to the Internet are writers—and many are successful at what they do.

Because of this renewed emphasis on written communication, all managers should be able to write and write well. There is no getting around it. What manager does not send memos to supervisors, colleagues, and staff; answer or initiate an endless stream of emails; take notes in meetings; write or edit reports and other documents; participate in the nearly forgotten yet essential art of letter writing; and accomplish that most dreaded of all managerial writing tasks—the performance review? These tasks require managers to spend a considerable part of their day communicating in written form.

If you've been hired as a manager, chances are you probably know how to write—at least a little. Good writing is clear, direct, and personal. But sadly, many business documents are convoluted. They use passive voice construction that sucks the life out of any narrative. Their prose seems written for some historical record rather than attempting to inform, persuade, or communicate. Don't let this happen to you!

## The Basics of Writing

In 1946, Eric Arthur Blair, better known by his pen name of George Orwell, wrote an essay called *Politics and the English Language*. In this essay he describes how written English has declined. Orwell, whose books *Animal Farm* and *1984* became required reading for high school and college students soon after they were published, wrote the essay because he felt that imprecise language had allowed the dictators of his day—Hitler and Stalin—to take power and keep it. He believed "the slovenliness of our language makes it easier for us to have foolish thoughts." This same criticism is leveled against Facebook and Twitter, more than 60 years later.

Orwell's essay offered six rules for good writing:

1. Never use a metaphor, simile, or other figure of speech that you are used to seeing in print.

2. Never use a long word where a short one will do.

3. If it is possible to cut a word out, always cut it out.

4. Never use the passive where you can use the active.

5. Never use a foreign phrase, a scientific word, or a jargon word if you can think of an everyday English equivalent.

6. Break any of these rules sooner than say anything outright barbarous (Orwell, 1946).

Orwell's rules pretty much sum up everything the average (and even the above-average) person should keep in mind when writing, but they are deceptively simple. Let's look at each in more detail.

**Never use a metaphor, simile, or other figure of speech that you are used to seeing in print.** A metaphor is an implied comparison between two nouns that are unlike each other, but have something in common. *My high school was torture.* A simile makes these comparisons explicit by adding the words "like" or "as." *Getting into this dance club is like getting into Lady Gaga's dressing room.*

Orwell's main point is for people to be original in their writing. The author, who died in 1950, would have been appalled to see what is on the Internet: People copy each other all the time. They either rehash information or outright plagiarize it. At the very least, information is repetitive and uninteresting. At the worst, it's illegal. It's essential that if you publish any writing, you know which content is original. But for managers, even if you aren't getting compensated for releasing writing to the public, you should keep in mind that employees are people too. They will want to read anything interesting, especially about work.

So how do you keep your own writing fresh? In memos, letters, and emails, you should *write like you talk.* Pretend you're having a conversation with your intended audience. If you're writing for a large audience, imagine a typical reader you'd like to convince, inform, or persuade. If that person was right in front of you, what would you say? Then write it.

**Never use a long word where a short one will do.** Many people think throwing big words around in a document makes you look smart. We could have said "demonstrates your erudition," but that would be less clear. Big words sometimes get in the way of your ability to communicate.

Your computer's thesaurus is very handy—type in a word and it will give you a list of similar words. But words rarely have exactly the same meaning, and some words are used better in different contexts. Reading widely will help you identify the context you need to make the proper word choice and will help you avoid awkward sentences. Don't repeat yourself; if a word appears more than three times in a paragraph, use a synonym. Check a dictionary if you don't understand the word a thesaurus provides. It may be just the word you're looking for.

Here's another hint: When choosing words, avoid those that sound too much like Latin. Latin is, of course, the root of the English language, but somehow, words that are closest to their Latin roots sound pretentious (see the examples in figure 3.1). Use Plain English whenever possible. If you're still in doubt, remember Orwell's original rule: Use the shorter word.

**If it is possible to cut a word out, always cut it out.** Here's where our rule of writing like you speak can get you into trouble. Lots of people use extra words in their speech— useless fillers that have no place in writing.

Just as people use filler words in speaking, writers also use filler words. One of the most frequently overused words is "that." As a word, it is sometimes necessary, but usually when it is before a noun. "I need that report tomorrow," is a good example. If it's placed after the noun, then it's unnecessary: "This is the report that our committee prepared." Some of the words have their place, but they make you sound indecisive and they weaken your writing.

**Figure 3.1**

Latin Words to Avoid

Here are some Latin words commonly used in business documents that can and should be avoided (from *Effective Writing Skills for Public Relations* by John Foster):

**Use**

- among others, not *inter alia*
- yearly or annually, not *per annum*
- about, not *circa*
- for this purpose, not *ad hoc*
- cause to effect, not *a priori*
- good faith, not *bona fide*
- let the buyer beware, not *caveat emptor*

- and others, not *et al*
- by virtue of an official position, not *ex officio*
- my fault, not *mea culpa*
- something given in compensation for something else, not *quid pro quo*.

Once you have eliminated filler words, you can move on to filler phrases. "I am writing to inform you" is a remnant of an older, more formal time. "At this point in time," can be: "Now." Think about the subtle meanings in words—people often add more words than necessary. If an adjective or adverb is already part of the word's meaning, cut it out. There are no "past records," just "records." Things do not need to be "eradicated completely," just eradicated. And there are no "old clichés," just "clichés." You should eliminate empty phrases from writing and speaking: "my bad," "you know what I mean," or "be proactive." Nearly everyone uses: "in my opinion." It is both unnecessary and weakening. Also avoid: "all things being equal." Take care to spell out words instead of using abbreviations, like "whatevs," or "no prob." These have no place in business communication, of course— even in informal emails.

**Figure 3.2**

Legal Jargon to Avoid

Here's a list of legal jargon words to avoid from the federal government's PlainLanguage.gov website. The list is based on the work of Professor Joseph Kimble, a legal writing scholar.

- above-mentioned
- aforementioned
- foregoing
- henceforth
- hereafter
- hereby
- herewith

- thereafter
- thereof
- therewith
- whatsoever
- whereat
- wherein
- whereof

**Never use the passive where you can use the active.** Active voice in writing means sentences are constructed with clear subject and action—the subject "acts." In the passive voice, the subject of the sentence is being acted upon. For example: "I read the report," and "The report was read by me." Active voice sentences are usually shorter. They are easier to understand. They offer punchiness—senior leadership is always looking for that when they hand back reports and tell you to "punch it up a little." Frequently, people confuse passive voice writing with formal writing—read any medical or law journal to know what formal writing means—but it isn't the same thing at all. If you want your writing to be direct, clear, and easy to read, edit all of your work to cut passive sentences.

As Orwell pointed out, however, sometimes sentences written in the passive voice have value—especially to the business writer. The famous apologetic phrase "mistakes were made" turns the liability of passive voice into a virtue because what the subject actually did was unclear, and because the actual subject is impossible to determine. When writers use that phrase, they avoid assigning responsibility for the problem.

Many academic journals do not allow contributors to use the word "I." In those cases, using passive voice is necessary. And sometimes, as Strunk and White point out, passive voice is necessary to make a particular word the subject of the sentence. But Orwell's fourth rule still applies in most cases: Whenever you can use active voice, do so.

**Never use a foreign phrase, a scientific word, or a jargon word if you can think of an everyday English equivalent.** As the PlainLanguage.gov site (a site dedicated to improving communication from the federal government to the public) describes it, avoid "unnecessarily complicated, technical language used to impress, rather than to inform, our audience."

---

**Figure 3.3**

### The Plain English Campaign

In England, the homeland of our language (the great playwright George Bernard Shaw once famously described the United States and Great Britain as "two nations separated by a common language"), the Plain English Campaign has been against gobbledygook, jargon, and misleading public information since 1979. They believe everyone should have access to clear and concise information, and their "Crystal Mark" is a guaranteed document written in Plain English.

They recommend these five basic written English techniques:

- an average sentence length of about 15-20 words
- the use of everyday English in business, such as words like "we" and "you" instead of "the insured" and "the applicant"
- conciseness
- an average line length of between seven and 23 words
- plenty of answer space and a logical flow on forms.

For more information and tips, visit their site at http://www.plainenglish.co.uk/

---

This is hard for many managers, who fail to understand that terms they use in conversation every day, such as "CPU," "the enterprise," and "myocardial infarction," are not understood in the same way by everyone—even if their only readers are also technical specialists. Define your terms whenever you use anything technical, and use acronyms as sparingly as possible, even when you've spelled the acronym out on first reference, because many people will not remember what you wrote two pages ago.

Jargon reduces accuracy, readability, and understandability—as does legal language such as "aforementioned," "henceforth," and "thereafter." And foreign phrases, even Latin ones like *ad hoc*, *et al*, and *quid pro quo*, should not be used when English equivalents are available. Your reader will think you are showing off, and may not understand what you are saying. You may think using foreign words gives your writing a good quality, but it really doesn't add much. That is, unless the words have no exact English equivalent, such as the Yiddish words *chutzpah* (referring to a certain type of shameless audacity); *schlemiel* (a person who is highly inept at everything); or *schlimazel* (someone who, if he didn't have bad luck, would have no luck at all). But it may take more time for you to use unfamiliar words and then explain them. Who needs extra confusion?

**Break any of these rules sooner than say anything outright barbarous.** Orwell lived and wrote these rules at a time when language was not only distorted to meet the service of the state, but was also a prime source in instigating and justifying mass murder. Writers manipulated ideas, misinformed their readers, and deliberately distorted the past—all of which Orwell believed destroyed freedom and a free society. His masterpiece, *1984*, described the logical outcome of the use of such tactics in the service of government.

Modern rhetoric is not as extreme as it was during World War II, when words were weapons of tremendous force. Still, as fewer people remain alive who lived through the momentous events of that era, that lesson is becoming extinct. The Internet has allowed extremist opinions of all sorts to get widespread attention.

For a manager, the objective is to be clearly understood. Don't embellish; don't point fingers; don't try to cleverly shift blame by using rhetorical devices. In short—be civil. If you must, write a draft that expresses your true emotions and then hit delete. Go back and rewrite your thoughts in a less emotional manner. You'll win more friends and influence more people that way—your staff and co-workers will be better for it.

## Editing Your Work

George Orwell was a journalist and a novelist. While his magazine writing seemed to go directly from his typewriter to the pages of the publications, he was much more painstaking with his novels. *1984* took three years to write, and he took the time to not only write the book, but also to edit it carefully. "The rough draft," he wrote to his publisher, "is always a ghastly mess bearing little relation to the finished result."

Most writers understand Orwell's description of a first draft as "a ghastly mess." Most nonwriters and managers, however, will not. The pain of writing is so great that the urge to get it over with causes them to hit the print button, or, worse yet, the send button. They should be carefully examining what they've written to see if it says what they mean it to say.

Whether you're writing an email to a subordinate or completing a 200-page report on the future of your company, take time to thoroughly review and edit your work before sending it. And since it is easier to spot problems in someone else's prose, offer to look over other people's work, so they will do so for you.

## EXPERT TIP

For more than 25 years, **Barbara Jacksier** edited decorating, crafts, and garden-ing magazines. As an editor, she looked for:

- **Stories with narratives**. Barbara's magazines featured stories with defined beginnings, middles, and ends—that made sense to readers all the way through. "I got rid of whatever didn't help tell the story, unless the digression was really interesting."

- **Openings that made readers want to keep reading**. According to Barbara, Susan Orlean is the contemporary author best at composing opening sentences.

- **Appropriate word style and language.** "Don't use the word 'cool' in a review of an opera," she explains.

- **Stories that 'sweat' the small stuff**. Consistent name spellings, quotes short and to the point, sentences no longer than they should be—writers who could do that consistently were worth their weight in gold.

It is, of course, a wonderful thing to have a professional editor review your work, but few—if any—workplaces offer that luxury. There's no reason, however, why you can't look at your own work a second time. Make sure your writing—even your brief emails—has a beginning, middle, and end. Start every communication in a way that keeps your reader interested. Keep your sentences brief, and don't forget to run your work through the spelling and grammar checker on your word processing program. Of course, most computer spell checkers will not spot a correctly spelled word that is in the wrong place.

Here are some final editing tips: first of all, **check your math**. Most documents prepared for business include figures of some kind. Sometimes they don't add up correctly or agree with other figures in the same document. Some bosses like nothing better than to use their calculators to trip up subordinates who have made mathematical errors; and they are right to do so, given that such mistakes can cost a firm millions of dollars!

Second, **don't trust the spelling or grammar checker to catch all of your mistakes**. Some typos are not caught because they spell a legitimate word but are not what you intended. Typing "pubic" instead of "public" has caused considerable embarrassment. Keep *The Elements of Style*, *The Associated Press Stylebook*, or Rudolf Flesch and A.H. Lass's great book *The Classic Guide to Better Writing* on your bookshelf.

You may also want to bookmark this site on your browser: *http://writing-program.uchicago. edu/resources/grammar.htm*. It's part of the University of Chicago Writing Program's website, and it's a gateway to some of the best grammar guides on the Internet; thesauruses more powerful than those on your word processing program; and writing on current grammatical thinking. (Grammar, as the site points out, is not like math; it continually evolves, and what is correct today may not be correct tomorrow.) The site is updated about four times a year, and they only recommend sites that are not boring or completely inundated with advertisements.

Third, and most important, **keep the ABCs in mind in both your writing and editing: Accuracy, Brevity, and Clarity**. Is what you're saying correct? Is it short? Is it clear? The British management analyst Owen Hargie once wrote: "The arteries of even the healthiest organization become clogged with paper. Readers therefore respond with gratitude toward short communication in which the primary point is nevertheless made clear (Hargie, Dixon, and Tourish, 1998)."

So remember that good writing is vigorous, direct, personal, and civil. Active voice is more powerful than passive voice. And accuracy, brevity, and clarity—as Napoleon understood—are the main tools of business writing. Follow these rules, and you'll be fine.

# WRITE EFFECTIVE LETTERS AND MEMORANDUMS

"If I had more time, I would have written a shorter letter."

—*T.S. Eliot*

---

### In This Chapter

- Why letters are still important.
- How to write a business letter.
- How to write a memo.
- How to write a report.

---

Even in this age of email, Twitter, and Facebook, the art of letter writing is one that managers still have to master. You may believe that love letters, thank-you notes, and correspondence with friends have gone the way of the cassette tape recorder. But business correspondence may be more important than ever. To some, it is the gold standard by which the quality of an organization's communication activity is judged. Knowing how to write and edit such correspondence properly is vital to accomplishing your present duties, and to your future success.

A 2004 survey conducted by The Business Roundtable found that two-thirds or more of salaried employees at most corporations have some responsibility for writing (The National Commission on Writing for America's Families, Schools, and Colleges, 2004). Except for the mining and transportation industries, large majorities of salaried employees in all industries are expected to write. And more than half of the companies responding to the survey say they frequently or almost always take writing skill into consideration when hiring salaried employees.

You may be an OK writer, but perhaps you can improve in the business writer's most basic tasks: how to write a business letter, memorandum, or report. But preparing a persuasive memorandum, writing standard operating procedures that are easy for subordinates to follow, drafting incident reports, or even answering a customer's written complaint may still fill you with fear.

You don't have to be creative to write a good business letter. In fact, that's exactly what you don't want to be. You want to be accurate, specific, and brief; your goal is to get your reader to understand you and to take the action you've suggested, or to accept the explanation you've provided. The bottom line—the point you make in whatever you write, and what you want readers to understand—is the key to your letter. You should get to that point quickly, because your readers must be told why there is value in continuing to read.

Perhaps business letters have fallen out of fashion in some places because they have certain disadvantages. Because they are not delivered instantaneously as emails are, you can't get immediate feedback from your recipient. If your letter raises questions or needs clarification, the issues can't be resolved right away. And, perhaps more importantly, poor writing is more obvious in a letter than it is in an email. A letter that is badly written reflects negatively on your company's reputation, while a poorly written email, in most cases, becomes acceptable as something done in haste.

Yet business letters survive, largely because their advantages far outweigh their disadvantages. First of all, written communication is permanent. Unlike electronic correspondence, a paper document provides an instant and permanent paper trail of your decisions and actions. If you are stating principles, policies, or rules, it's far better to write them down in a letter than in an email—a process subject to instant deletion. And writing for paper requires the valuable discipline of taking your time to think about what you're writing and writing exactly what you mean. In musical terms, think of emails as the equivalent of rappers making up words as they perform. Letters are compositions that are understood in a standardized way. Both have their place, and managers must know how to write well in both situations, and when to use each.

## The Parts of a Letter

Many large organizations have correspondence guides that describe how people should write letters on company stationery. Even if you work in one of those organizations, there are likely to be times when you can't consult the manual. And if you don't work for an organization that has a manual, you'll need some help. For your ready reference, here are pointers for how a letter should be organized.

At the very top of the letter is the *letterhead*, which identifies your company and provides the address where any return correspondence should be sent.

Right beneath the address at the left margin, put the *date* on which you've written the letter or the date you intend for it to be mailed—whichever is later. You'd be amazed at how important the date is—people file your letter using it; it's a great way to avoid confusion in responses ("In your April 23 letter, you said..."); and it's a reminder to your correspondent that her reply is timely or not—so please, do not omit the date.

Some people add a reference line below the date, which is useful when you're writing to a large company and don't know to whom to send your letter, or if you're answering a specific letter. This is also a good place for reference numbers, such as a case number or purchase order number.

Next comes the *name and address* of the person to whom you are writing. In many large offices, most mail is opened by someone other than the addressee, and sometimes the envelope gets lost in the transfer—which is why you have to put the name and address inside, too, to make sure the letter gets where it's supposed to go.

After that comes the *salutation*, or greeting, a traditional ritual followed by letter writers for hundreds of years. In business letters, the salutation almost always begins with "Dear," and is followed by either "Ms. Smith," or "John" or "Sir or Madam" or some variation on one of those themes. Follow the salutation with a colon—not a comma.

Some people include a *subject line* to follow the salutation (don't bother if you've already inserted a reference line below the date.) Emails, which almost always have subjects, have influenced letters because in the past letters did not have subject lines. Subject lines help your reader know, at a glance, what your letter's about. If you use one, keep it short. Finally, you get to the *body* of the letter. We'll discuss this in more detail below.

After the body of text, end your letter with a closing. This is a phrase like "Sincerely," or "Very truly yours," or "Best regards." If your organization doesn't specify the phrase to use in your closing, pick something that reflects the tone of your letter, as long as it's respectful.

Leave five blank lines after that and type in your name. As a manager, you should put your title and your company name on lines under your name. Of course, the blank space is for you to sign your name—so that whoever gets the letter knows you've at least seen it, even if you ascend far enough up the ranks that someone else writes your letters for you.

## The Body of a Business Letter

Even if you skipped over the previous section because your current company has a style manual that determines what all letters will look like, here's the part you should not skip—unless you want to write lots more cover letters before your next promotion. What makes a good business letter? It's a letter that:

- **Is brief:** People don't have time to read long letters anymore. Ask yourself the question: "What do I want my audience to do or to know after reading this letter?" Then answer that question as close to the beginning of the letter as possible.

- **Is warm and friendly, not cold and impersonal:** Part of the goal of most business letters is not only to convey information, but also to build a business relationship. A letter filled with legalisms, fancy words, or Latin phrases will not be perceived as an example of your extraordinary intellect or vocabulary. It will only appear pretentious and wordy. The KISS acronym "keep it short and simple," originated in the design community, but it applies here.

**Figure 4.1**

A Sample Business Letter


The Balmy Lip Balm Company
123 Sunny Day Lane
Key West, FL 33040


Ms. Angelina Jolie
The Mansion On The Hill
Beverly Hills, CA 90210


Subject: Our new lip balm product

Dear Ms. Jolie:


Thank you for your letter praising our company's former lip balm product. The reason you can no longer find the old version of Balmy's Lip Balm in Beverly Hills, California is because we are in the process of replacing it with a newer version we are confident you will appreciate and enjoy.

The rumor you have heard is true: We will be replacing the secret ingredient in our formula. This is because bats are becoming an endangered species, and it was increasingly difficult to obtain sufficient quantities of the bat waste by-product we were using. (Of course, we would never harm any actual bats!)

I hope you will agree that our new synthetic formula lip balm, which uses no human or animal product or waste material, will be as good as, if not better than, our previous product. I am enclosing a free sample of the new Balmy's Lip Balm, so you can see for yourself just how good it is. I am sure the career successes you attribute to our old lip balm will continue once you've tried our new one.

Thank you for being such a good customer in the past, and enjoy the sample!


Sincerely,


I.M. Balmy
President, Balmy Lip Balm

- **Is written at an appropriate level of familiarity:** In making the letter friendly, you have to consider your audience. The person you write to also plays an important part in determining the tone of your letter. You can be more familiar, of course, with someone you know than with a stranger, but you must also write differently to your boss than to your colleagues or to anyone who reports to you.

- **Is organized in a logical manner:** In every good letter—in fact every good written document—sentence follows sentence in a logical way, just as B follows A. Don't jump around between topics. If you introduce more than one concept, make sure you've completed your discussion of the first topic before you move on to the second.

- **Is persuasive:** In most cases, you will ask your readers to take some action after they read what you have to say. You need to persuade or educate them to take the action you want. Provide them with the information they need to agree with you, presented in a logical and factual manner.

- **Emphasizes the positive:** Avoid using negative words such as can't, won't, and impossible. Instead, a good letter emphasizes what you can do. Instead of "We no longer make those widgets," try "Although our popular widget model A-123 is sold out, we have a new model A-124 that may fit your needs. I've enclosed a product brochure that describes its features."

- **Uses the writing skills described in chapter 3:** Always write using active voice, not passive; keep your words short; cut whatever you can; avoid jargon and foreign phrases; and above all, be courteous. Even if you're writing a complaint letter, or responding to an angry customer who, in your opinion, is way off base—keep your cool. You can, indeed, catch more flies with honey than with vinegar, and even if your objective in writing is something other than catching flies, being civil in your correspondence is the right thing to do for your company and your own reputation.

Before starting to write, think of a one-sentence description of what you hope to accomplish through your words. Use that description to create your first draft—and then pare down the draft to what is essential. Don't put that description in your letter. Review your logic, check vocabulary for readability and negativity, proofread carefully, confirm the gender of your recipient, and send it out. Of course, if others draft letters for your review or signature, it's doubly important you look for all these things before giving your approval, since your staff may not have the same point of view as yours. You may have to send many letters back for a while, marked up with your corrections, but eventually your staff will figure out what you're looking for.

## Writing Memos

Writing coaches and college business courses focus most on letter writing, but it is the humble memo, or memorandum, that still makes the business world go around. Memos can be addressed to a group of people. Even when they are addressed to one person, there will be other readers. A well-written memo can make or break a career. It actually did for one of us. As a brand new government employee, Ev wrote a memo on the operating hours of a lock and dam in Troy, New York, and got noticed by senior leadership as someone who could make a coherent argument in writing.

**EXPERT TIP**

As the director of executive correspondence for a large government agency, **Katrice Pasteur** and her staff of 12 review between 5–10,000 letters, memos, and reports every year. "Letters are still extremely important in business," she says. According to Katrice, a good letter:

- **Addresses all of the correspondent's concerns, without dancing around the issues**. "Get to the bottom-line issues in the beginning—and make sure the writer doesn't have to write back again and tell you that you didn't answer his question."

- **Doesn't beat around the bush**. If the answer is no, it's no. "And don't try to overwhelm your correspondence with information they didn't ask for, either—that just invites them to write back again and ask more questions."

- **Is consistent with other correspondence you've written**. "It's OK to say the same thing to different people."

Typically, memos are to the point. Most memos do one of four things: they provide information or directions to their readers; they record agreements between groups (these are often called "memorandums of agreement" or "memorandums of understanding"); they allow an action to take place; or they make an argument in favor of, or opposed to, a course of action. To maintain clarity and directness, you should limit the number of points you make in a memo. If you have several points to make, you should separate them into more than one memo, or call for a meeting.

Because memos are usually internal documents, they are more informal than letters but are more formal than emails. Also, because they are internal, most organizations have templates for preparing them. If you're managing a small business, however, and develop your own forms and procedures, Microsoft Word has several memo templates you can use. They include a:

**To:** line, in which you enter the name of the memo's principal audience, or the group or organization it is being sent to.

**From:** line, in which you enter your name, your title, or both.

**Date:** line, in which you enter the date (but you knew that, didn't you)?

**Subject:** or **Re:** (for reference) line, in which you explain the subject of your memo. Take time to write a subject that will get the attention of your reader, while still being appropriate. With all the emails today's business executive receives, and all the letters and other information they read, your memo needs to stand out. So make sure the subject line interests them.

**Figure 4.2**

A Sample Memorandum


To: All Organization Members

From: Avon Barksdale, Chief Executive

Date: August 15, 2012

Subject: Appointment of Stringer Bell as Acting Chief Executive

As many of you know, I have recently been called out of town on a special assignment. While I am endeavoring to return to headquarters as quickly as possible, and will remain in touch with the organization via phone, email, and occasional face-to-face meetings, I believe it is necessary to appoint someone to manage the day-to-day aspects of our organization while I am away.

Accordingly, I have asked Russell 'Stringer' Bell to assume the role as Acting Chief Executive during the period of my absence. Stringer has been my right-hand man in the past, and is fully familiar with all aspects of our operation. In addition, he and I will consult on a regular basis, so you may assume that any direction he provides has my full approval.

I hope you will provide Stringer with the same level of cooperation and loyalty you have provided me in the past. As I have only a limited capability to receive phone calls and emails on my current assignment, please contact him directly if you have any questions regarding this memo, or any other subject.


Thank you for your continued support,


Avon Barksdale

---

The body of the memo follows the subject line. What you put in the body depends on your purpose for writing the memo.

- If you're *providing information* to your readers, it's usually to help them make a decision. Give them good, solid information, simply presented. As a manager, it's your job to present not only the good news, but also the bad. Don't bury the truth under an avalanche of words. Remember the letter will be a permanent record. Try to anticipate what your readers already know. It's no use to anyone to go into detail about general, easy issues. If you do, they won't read what's really important.

- If you're *recording an agreement*, be comprehensive. Make sure to include all the pertinent details. In the future, it will be an important record, and will be used when there are questions about what each party in the agreement actually meant.

- If you're *allowing something to take place*, be especially brief. "Effective June 1, Jane Jones will be acting director of our Marketing Division," tells readers all they need to know (unless, of course, you want to add a brief biography of Jane to introduce her).

- If you're *making an argument*, which is the most difficult form of memo writing, keep your writing simple, so your argument is understood. Summarize your argument in the first paragraph—not the last—so readers understand right away what you're thinking and can follow your thoughts clearly. Make transitions from one step of your argument to the next; order your thoughts in a logical manner (using topic headings can help you do that); and write a conclusion that sums up everything you said and what you want readers to do.

Many people use numbers or bulleted lists to make the information they present easily accessible. Whether you use these or not, you should write short, concise paragraphs. The usual writing rules apply for any memo, especially about using active voice, using easy-to-follow vocabulary, and being civil. In memos about assigning responsibility, make sure it's clear to whom those responsibilities have been assigned.

For many years, it was commonly accepted practice in memos to close without a signature or a closing other than "For additional information, please contact..." Nowadays, many people sign off on their memos, either with a signature above their typed name or with a close like "Sincerely." Remember that in a memo, your title is in the From: line, so it's different from letter writing, where your title is at the bottom with your typed name and signature. It is a good new trend to sign memos.

As a manager, you should read all the memos you receive carefully—not only for their content, but also to help you conform memos you write to the organization's accepted style. And keep this last rule in mind: If you're writing to an outside organization, use a letter; if it's within the organization, write a memo; and if your memo is more than two pages long, consider a report instead.

## Writing Reports

Whatever your writing skill level, at some point in your career you will have to write a report. Not to put more pressure on this task, but a well-written, useful report can make or break a career. The poorly written report exposes flaws in a manager's ability to write and flaws in that person's entire thinking process.

There are, in general, three types of reports: those that provide information, those that analyze situations or trends, and those that make recommendations for action. Whatever the reason for the report's preparation, a good report should always be *well-written*, so it holds the interest of its intended reader. It should be *factual*, so avoid slanting your arguments by omitting pertinent facts that contradict your thesis. It should be *well-organized*, so readers who only have time to skim its contents will still understand what you say; and it should be *well-presented*, using an easy-to-read typeface, short paragraphs, bold headings, simple graphs and charts, wide margins, and lots of white space. Every report should have the following sections:

- An **introductory section**, with a cover, title page, table of contents, list of illustrations and attachments, and an executive summary. The executive summary briefly presents what the report is about, its most important recommendations, and the implications the report will have for the future of your company. You may also want to provide an **abstract**, which summarizes the report in about 200 words or less.

- An **actual introduction**, which explains why the report is written, and to help your audience follow the argument you will make.

- A **findings section** (or the main body of the report), which describes the information and facts you want your readers to know about.

- Your **conclusions**, where you lay out what you have learned from the facts in the preceding section. This is not the place for you to offer your readers any new facts or information they haven't previously seen.

- Your **recommendations**, which should be entirely based on your conclusions.

Some reports also include sections on **methodology**, in which you describe how your research was done; **acknowledgements**, in which you thank all those who contributed to the report's preparation; **appendices** for those interested in additional information, especially source materials you relied on in preparing the report; and **references**, essentially a bibliography of all the sources you consulted.

In the research phase before writing a report, first make sure you understand your audience, and the precise purpose of your report. Then, make sure you fully understand the way things are now: Many reports have gone way off track because they did not understand the current situation, leading to imperfect predictions of the future.

Collect as much data as you can, including information about performance and production, and—if applicable—information about current costs. Make it as easy as possible to understand the data you've collected by using charts, graphs, numbered lists, and bullet points (all of which are easy to do in Microsoft Word). Finally, as you consider your recommendations, be goal-oriented, and make your language explicit. Write in terms like "10 percent increases," or "30 percent reductions in cost." Then figure out what you need to do to get there, and develop those thoughts into your recommendations.

Try not to make too many recommendations. Keep in mind the basic question of what your organization can do differently to deal with the issue you have outlined—and how what you recommend will change things for the better.

# COMPOSE EMAILS THAT GET ACTION

"Diamonds are forever. Email comes close."

—*June Kronholz*

---

### In This Chapter

- How to communicate properly by email.
- How to avoid misunderstandings in email.
- How to preserve your sanity and your personal space in an avalanche of emails.

---

Electronic mail, or email, a communication technique that's barely 40 years old, has become ubiquitous in today's society. It's easy to see why; sending an email is much faster and cheaper than mailing a letter. While a phone call must be answered immediately, an email can be put aside, read, and responded to at the recipient's leisure—resulting in minimal disruptions to everyone's schedule. And you can send an email to virtually anyone, anytime, anywhere in the world.

Most managers receive a tidal wave of emails. It's not unusual for a manager to receive hundreds of emails per day. This deluge can take over your life and keep you from doing things—like supervising staff—managers are paid to do. Receiving hundreds of emails daily can wreak havoc on your personal life as well, so that nights, weekends, and holidays are all held hostage to the smartphone.

Since emails are delivered at breathtaking speed over tens of thousands of miles, there is a difference in the way they are perceived and used. Because they are received so quickly, and responses sometimes provided just as fast, they are more conversational and less formal in nature than any paper-based form of communication. Since they are informal, they do not require the same standards of writing that formal documents do.

---

**Figure 5.1**

Eye-Popping Email Numbers

Here are some statistics from the Radicati Group's 2011 Report:

- In 2011, there were 3.1 billion email accounts throughout the world, 2.6 billion instant messaging accounts, and 2.4 billion social networking accounts. Only 14 percent of email users live and work in North America, however. Nearly half the world's users live in the Asia-Pacific area. The Radicati Group expects an average annual growth rate in email accounts of 7 percent so that there will be nearly 4.1 billion email accounts by the end of 2015.

- Three-quarters of all email accounts are "owned" by consumers; only 25 percent of mailboxes are corporate email accounts. Corporate accounts are expected to increase faster than consumer accounts over the next few years, however.

- The typical corporate email user sends and receives about 105 email messages every day (sending 33 and receiving 72). Growth in this area is slowing due to the rapid rise in instant messaging and social networks. About 19 percent of email messages delivered to corporate email users are spam.

- Thanks to smartphones and other advancements, more than 531 million people now send email wirelessly, and that number is expected to increase to more than 1.2 billion by the end of 2015.

---

But well-regarded managers don't take this more relaxed tone as an excuse to throw out the rules of proper grammar and spelling when preparing emails.

Although emails are more conversational than letters, they are still no substitute for real conversations. You can't infer tone, facial expression, gestures, and vocal inflection from an email. You may think the person to whom you are writing knows you're kidding about something, but you may be disastrously wrong. And sarcasm, which is very much a part of everyday conversation, is difficult to discern in an email.

People don't often consider another interesting aspect of email; unlike a letter, a report, or even a spoken conversation, what you write may not be in the same form as what your recipient sees. When you have a conversation, all the parties involved hear the same voices; when you write a letter or report, everyone sees the same document, with font and formatting in the same way. But different email programs, such as Microsoft Outlook and Apple Mail, process messages differently—so what your recipient sees on her screen may not appear in the same format you so carefully developed, especially if they're reading your message on a handheld device.

We use email for personal communication and for work, so it can be confusing. It's usually pretty clear whether a physical letter is a business or personal communication. A letter sprayed with perfume and decorated with hearts and flowers tells you something about its content immediately. And we have a sense that letters are permanent, but emails are ephemeral, so most people try harder to be grammatically correct when writing letters. Thanks to modern storage technology, emails may be as permanent as letters, and are a lot easier to find when you need them.

And there's that "Send" button, patiently waiting to immediately deliver electrons to the office down the hall or thousands of miles away. It's so easy, so quick, and so final. We have time to reflect on letters and reports—even if only the time it takes to find a stamp, address an envelope, and take the letter to a mailbox. But emails don't encourage any kind of reflection. They are designed to provide speed, even when you are hurtling toward destroying your own career with a poorly-worded, intemperate, or just plain stupid communication.

How do you avoid these traps and communicate properly using this valuable, but potentially dangerous, new medium?

## Email Etiquette

The choices you have before you even begin writing an email are critical to your ability to get your point across. Every email begins with a To: line, in which you provide the address of your intended recipient. Sounds simple enough, right? But if you send an email to too many people, everyone will figure it's someone else's responsibility to respond or do what you asked. When that happens, of course, nothing gets done. Try sending out an email like this and see what happens:

To: Gryffindor Team
From: Oliver Wood, Captain
Subject: Bringing the Butterbeer

Will someone please remember to bring a few bottles of butterbeer for a celebration after our Quidditch match tomorrow? Thanks!

Without a specific tasking, it's likely no one will take responsibility for the job. Send the message to the person you ask to accomplish the task, and put everyone else on the cc: line. Also, if you thank someone for their work, or for any reason, put only that person on the To: line, and cc: everyone else.

Here's something else to keep in mind when you send a message to several people: You give each person the email addresses of all the others. That's fine when you send a message to a group of friends, or within your organization—but be careful when you write to a group of people who don't know each other. You need to be about as careful with people's email addresses as you are with other personal information; maybe more so, given the proliferation of spammers these days. And finally, rank has its privileges, even in emails. Put the most senior person first, whenever seniority or status is an issue.

Be careful of when your email program automatically suggests recipients as you type in the first few letters of names. If more than one person in your book shares the same first name, it's easy to click on the wrong one and send your message to someone else.

Cc: stands for carbon copy, or for courtesy copy. Use the cc: line to keep people in the loop about things, with the understanding that no action is required from them. If you are part of an email string, you can also use the cc: line to bring people into the loop who were originally excluded but who should be aware of the discussion. But always explain that you have done so in the body of the message: *I am adding Professor Snape to the list to ensure he is aware that we will be drinking butterbeer after the match.* When responding to an email, if you are in doubt about including someone on the cc: line who was not originally a part of the message, proper etiquette is to ask the originator.

If you add someone to a cc: line, it can change the importance of a message. If you reprimand or compliment a subordinate, adding your own boss to the message adds considerable weight to the message. Copying a third party of importance—like a reporter, a member of Congress, or someone from the Department of Consumer Affairs—also lends weight to the message. Used in this way, the cc: line becomes a powerful—but dangerous—tool.

The bcc: or blind courtesy copy line is another tool that should be used carefully. When you use the bcc: line, the recipient of your message does not know that you have sent it to the person you have bcc'd it to. This is somewhat devious, so use the tool very carefully. One legitimate way to use bcc: is when you are sending messages to large groups of unrelated people, so they are not given the addresses of the others on the list, thereby protecting everyone's privacy.

Bcc:s are also useful in keeping legal counsel or other influential people aware of what you are doing in certain situations. This keeps the other side from knowing you are consulting with your lawyers, which otherwise might put them more on their guard. Of course, in such situations, they are likely doing the same thing. An alternative to bcc'ing someone is simply to forward them a message with "FYI" in the body of the message.

The From: line is straightforward, but, as the book *Send* points out, you should consider the email address from which you send a message (Shipley and Schwalbe, 2007). Use a private email address to send out resumes. Send your business emails from your business address, and your personal emails from a personal account. If you're self-employed, you should have an account for each purpose.

Finally, there's the Subject: line. This is the single most important line in any email message. It explains why the recipient should open your email. This is not a trivial matter: Leaders who receive more than 300 emails a day decide whether to open them or not by glancing at the subject. Many will forward emails to someone else based on the subject line alone. If you want to persuade your readers to take action, the subject line is essential. Plus, subject lines are a great way to organize your thoughts and your message. If what you write doesn't relate to your message's subject, you need to edit your message, choose a different subject line, or write another message.

## The Body of the Email

Emails are less formal than letters, that's true. They are best used to transmit short bits of information: the time of the meeting, who will be there, which subjects will be covered. When writing an email, the most important thing to keep in mind is this: Keep it as short as possible. Most of us have experienced replies to our emails that indicate the sender didn't read all the way through. In the age of hundreds of emails per day, people simply don't have time to read long emails. Even if you write beautiful, layered prose, you're still susceptible to people who don't read your work.

**Figure 5.2**

### Choose a Subject for Your Email

Here are some rules for choosing a subject line that will get people's attention:

- **Don't leave it blank.** It's pretty arrogant in a business situation for you to think someone will open a message just because it has your name on it. That's what you're asking them to do when you leave the subject line blank. Give your reader a reason to look at what you send.

- **Don't use generic phrases.** A message with a subject like "Important: please read," or "FYI," or even "Great News" is not giving your reader much more to work with than if the subject line were blank. What's important or urgent to you may not be anywhere near as important to your reader. And save "Great news" for really great news, or else you'll make your reader angry. A message with the phrase "quick question" in it has the same problem: If the question is so quick, why not just put it in the subject line? These generic subject lines also make it harder for you to find specific messages, so try to include a descriptive word or two.

- **Keep it short.** As *Send* points out, many people check their emails on smartphones and other handheld devices. There isn't much room for a subject line on those devices, so if you write a long subject line, they're only going to see a truncated version.

- **Be descriptive.** Tell people what they're in for: What are you going to say in the body of the message? Besides enticing people to read what you've written, there's another important reason not to be vague in the subject line. If your subject is "The item you requested," it may not get past the spam blocker! Also, a descriptive subject line helps your recipient find your email when searching for it.

- **Use EOM (end of message) or NRN (no reply necessary).** If you've really got a quick question, why not just make that the subject of your message? Adding EOM—for end of message—is a great courtesy to your recipient. It means she doesn't have to even open the email to know what you want—and, as an added bonus, it gets her thinking about your request right away. Adding NRN keeps additional useless messages from clogging up your inbox that simply say "Thank you," or "Okay."

In the past few years, the 140-character limit set by Twitter and the 420-character limit for Facebook status updates have conditioned millions of email users to say what we have to say more quickly. The Twitter limit may be a little short for many business uses, but what if we all tried to limit ourselves to the Facebook limit? Figure out what you want to say; put as much of it as possible in your first sentence; don't ask your readers to answer a lot of questions (if you do, they won't); and offer useful information in as few words as possible. Remember, you're not the only one overwhelmed by the many emails you get.

Because they are brief—or should be—it is difficult to get the tone right. Different businesses find many tones acceptable. You can be more informal in your emails if you work for Ben & Jerry's Ice Cream than if you work for the Securities and Exchange Commission. Since different types of messages require different tones, you must make sure the tone of your message is not subject to misinterpretation.

**Reminder 5.1**

**Emoticons:** an entirely new symbolic language designed to make sure readers get the joke, or understand that a sentence is ironic and not to be taken literally.

According to Wikipedia, emoticons are "facial expressions pictorially represented by punctuation and letters, usually expressing a writer's mood."

A happy face ☺

A frowning face ☹

Emoticons may not be suitable for business purposes, so don't be the only one in your office using them. And around the world, writing a sentence in all caps is the equivalent of shouting.

Here are some other tips that can help you write emails clear enough to read:

**Assume the reader will only read the first line, and skim everything else.** Make it easy for them. Write short paragraphs. Use bullets and subheads.

**Get your spelling and grammar right.** As a manager of others, you need to set an example. Writing poorly reflects badly on you. If you need more help in learning to write than what you found in this book, then get it. Writing classes are available online and in person. If you can write well enough but think that using email allows you to write in the shorthand people now use in text and Twitter messages, you're wrong—unless your message is sent to very close friends. This could change, however. For now, don't use them. Poor grammar and spelling don't inspire confidence in a manager. In this age of spelling and grammar checkers, there's no excuse for sending a message with significant errors.

**Reminder 5.2**

Phrases from texting are entering more general usage:

- BFN (bye for now)
- F2F (face to face)
- AFAIK (as far as I know)

There's precedent for this—the World War II generation gave us "snafu" (situation normal, all [fouled] up).

**Stick to the facts.** Henry Ford, the founder of the Ford Motor Company, was attributed the phrase: "Don't explain, and don't complain." You don't have to make sure your readers understand the background behind every message you send; they just need to quickly grasp the main point. In nearly every case, readers don't care about anything else.

**Keep the compliments to a minimum.** You're not going to get your reader to do what you want with excessive compliments. Most people see through that kind of false flattery. If you mean it, say it. Otherwise, it's not worth it.

**Don't use attachments if you don't have to.** We're guessing that many people who receive attached documents don't take time to open them. And when they get multiple attachments, the likelihood they open and read them decreases significantly. Attachments are difficult and sometimes impossible to read on smartphones. If there's something in a document that has to be read, why not cut and paste it from the document into your message? Also, if you have to use attachments, give them descriptive names, so it's clear what's in them before opening. A file titled "40001982908.pdf," is no help.

**Use a readable font and appropriate font size.** Twelve-point type is best, and is what most people use. Use larger type only if writing to someone who is visually impaired; never use type sizes below 10 points. If you don't know a good font to use, try Arial. Keep it simple. There are many interesting fonts available for emailers to use, and they're fine for personal messages, but they distract from the content of a business email. They also make the message hard to read, which is just what you try to avoid.

**Orwell's rules still apply.** In chapter 3, we described George Orwell's six rules for writing well: be original; use short words instead of long; cut words whenever you can; avoid the passive voice; avoid foreign phrases, scientific words, and jargon whenever possible; and, above all, be civil. All of these apply to email, especially the need for civility. Legendary "flame wars," in which all parties to an email string search for more inventive ways to insult one another, may be fun to read, but they do nothing to enhance the reputations of those who participate. The "send" button may be convenient—but be very careful before you send a message that is disparaging in any way, even if that person or group of people is not your message's intended recipient.

## Manage Your Email Inbox

Learning how to write emails properly is not the only thing to know about electronic communication. There's also the task of managing the tidal wave of emails every manager receives on a daily basis. If left unchecked, these emails can swamp everything a manager does. Reading and answering emails takes up time that can be used for interacting with other employees, working on teams, and even family time. The ability to read emails 24/7 has led—perhaps inevitably—to an expectation that people are available at all times to read and respond to business emails.

In their book *The Hamster Revolution*, authors Mike Song, Vicki Halsey, and Tim Burress offer a plan "to manage your email before it manages you." They recommend to:

**Reduce the volume of emails you receive by sending fewer emails yourself.** Question whether emails are actually needed, appropriate to send (professional and inoffensive), and targeted to the right people. Limit the number of people you cc: on an email to those who actually need to read the message, and others will follow suit.

**Improve the quality of the emails you send**, by using focused subject lines and short, to-the-point body text.

**Teach others to email properly**, by convincing them that reductions in email volume will increase their own productivity.

**Use a system to file and store your emails**, so you can find them more easily. The authors suggest a COTA system to organize your email folders (first Clients, then Output (your team's products and services), then Teams, then Administration (non-core job responsibilities), but whatever works for you is better than having hundreds of messages sitting unfiled and unsorted in your inbox (Song, Halsey, and Burress, 2007).

### EXPERT TIP

**Dr. Michael J. Kussman**, a physician who is also a retired U.S. Army General, is known among his colleagues and subordinates for his ability to respond quickly and efficiently to the many emails he receives every day. His tips include:

- **Don't let your emails pile up unread.** "Whenever I had five or 10 minutes, I'd read and answer a few—and when I had lunch at my desk, I'd answer emails while I ate."

- **Prioritize the emails you receive.** First, read those addressed directly to you. Then read those on which you are cc'd. "I'd say about 10–20 percent of the emails I received were important, but you have to be careful because you never know when a message that seems unimportant now can become important in the future."

- **Keep your emails short**, and encourage others to do the same.

- **Don't put anything in writing you wouldn't want someone else to read**, whether or not he is an addressee.

- **If you feel uncomfortable, think before hitting send.** "Ask yourself several times if it's OK. I'd say I ended up not sending about half of the messages I wrote that I was concerned about."

## Final Thoughts

Emails are great for sending important information quickly; they can be sent almost anywhere in the world at any time; and they are delivered virtually at the speed of light. But despite their ubiquitous presence in our society, they may not always be the right way for a manager to communicate with others. The phone is still a powerful communication tool. One phone call can often take the place of a dozen emails; nuances of tone can be heard in people's voices; and there's a greater likelihood that your message will be kept private and unrecoverable.

Face-to-face discussions may be more important than ever. Taking the time to visit someone else's office these days is a gesture of respect and interest. As an added bonus, you get to see the other person's reactions and body language to what you're saying, and you can adjust your own thinking and position accordingly. If you want more information about email usage, see the book *Send: The Essential Guide to Email for Office and Home*, by David Shipley and Will Schwalbe. It's the authoritative source on emails, their history, and their use. *Send* offers this golden rule for the 21st century: Never do anything electronically that you would want others to do to you in person (Shipley and Schwalbe, 2007).

Before emails, we were not as productive. Since emails have entered the workplace, our productivity has increased a hundredfold, but that productivity is threatened by overuse and burnout. Be judicious in your own use of email; limit your on-duty use to business. Keep your messages short and your points clear, and you can successfully harness the tremendous power of this essential business tool.

CHAPTER 6

# WRITE FOR THE WEB

"The simpler you say it, the more eloquent it is."

—*August Wilson*

---

### In This Chapter

- How we read on the web.
- How to write for the web.
- How to keep your writing objective, skimmable, and concise.

---

In 1997, the Internet was still in its infancy. Neither Amazon nor Google existed. Facebook founder Mark Zuckerberg was in middle school. And the concept that computers could make high-definition videos available on-demand to anyone was a technological achievement no one believed would happen anytime soon.

Webpages—sites available to everyone with Internet access who want to read them—were still relatively new in 1997. That was the year, in fact, that the number of websites reached one million. (By 2011, there were more than two billion). In that year, Sun Microsystems engineers Dr. John Morkes and Dr. Jakob Nielsen conducted a seminal study on how people read on the web. The Internet and the way we use it has changed tremendously in the years since this study was first published. However, Morkes and Nielsen's work remains the basis for the way most writing for the web is done.

After testing pioneer Internet users, the researchers came to three conclusions. First, they suggested people do not actually read on the Internet; they instead skim the pages they've navigated to, and pick out only a few sentences or even parts of sentences to get the information they want. Second, Internet users don't like long, scrolling pages; they want writers to get to the point. And third, users vastly prefer factual information to anything that seems like "marketing fluff (Morkes and Nielsen, 1997)." Concisely written websites scored 58 percent higher in measured usability (the ability of readers to find what they're looking for) when writing was brief, compared to the typical website. Sites written with "skimmable" text scored 47 percent higher in usability, and those written in an "objective style" scored 27 percent higher than the "promotional style" most webpages used then.

Morkes and Nielsen wrote their study at a time when writing for the web was a specialized art. Both men continue to write and publish in this area, and Dr. Nielsen publishes a monthly newsletter on how to make websites more usable for readers. At that time, it was recognized that the Internet was a means to allow large numbers of people to express themselves in writing for general and specialized audiences. But not many people took advantage of that opportunity at the time. Today, however, simply maintaining your own Facebook page or active Twitter account gives you access to a potentially huge audience.

Few managers will maintain their company Facebook page or Twitter account. You are likely, however, to write for the web on behalf of your organization at some point in your career—to provide information about the company, or to help your company increase or improve its business. You may be asked to contribute to your organization's webpage by explaining what your department does. You may need to provide content for a website related to one of your projects. Or you may contribute a blog post to your company's blog—or perhaps create a blog yourself, for your customers and potential customers, your staff, or your fellow employees.

Your company may also have an Intranet system: a system that can be accessed by everyone within the company, but no one outside. Intranets are great because they create a sense of community within an organization; train staff; let people know what's going on where they work; keep field staff and telecommuters involved; and improve the ability of managers to communicate with employees.

Whatever the reason you may need to write for the web, keep Morkes and Nielsen's three findings in mind to help you communicate better: keep it concise, keep it skimmable, and keep it objective. Figure 6.1 offers some ideas to help you do this.

## Write a Blog

If you're asked to write a blog post, don't feel overwhelmed. A blog is an easy way to keep clients and others informed about what's going on in your business. Most companies use blogs to make announcements or to help roll out new products and services. Blogs are a sales tool, and a way to make new and old clients feel more comfortable with you and your company. As the Internet has evolved, blogs have become more popular and more credible, and are widely read by Internet users.

Successful blogs start conversations between authors and readers, and among the readers themselves. Write about what you know, in as conversational a manner as you can, on subjects you believe your audience would like to know more about. Let them know what action you want them to take as a result of reading your post, and be clear about it. Be personal and objective. Forget the "happy talk" and get to the point. A good way to conclude any blog is by asking a question. "What do you think?," "How would you have responded?," or "Where should we go from here?" are often used.

**Figure 6.1**

A Checklist for Web Writers

- **Use headlines that grab people's attention**. You must use strong verbs and adjectives. Don't title an article, "10 Rules for Writing for the Web." Instead, try "10 Foolproof Web-Writing Rules." Also, try to get the headline to explain the topic well, such as "Seven Simple Steps to Become a Better Leader." Just as a newspaper or magazine headline writer does, you can say something controversial in a headline to grab your readers' attention, ask an interesting question, or make a comparison between two points of view.

- **Keep your paragraphs and sentences short**. On the Internet, if your paragraphs are longer than five lines, and your individual sentences are more than one line, they're probably too long. One way to shorten sentences is to limit your use of punctuation marks, especially colons and semicolons. If your sentence requires a colon or a semicolon, split the sentence in two. Leave lots of white (blank) space around paragraphs, by using wide margins and double-spacing between paragraphs.

- **Don't try to write for everyone**. You've got a target audience: maybe it's your staff and co-workers; your clients; or potential clients. You can't be all things to all people, so concentrate on whom you're trying to reach.

- **Think like a journalist**. Just about the first thing an aspiring reporter is taught in school is the inverted pyramid style. In this style, the most important information in the story is placed in the first paragraph; the second most important in the second paragraph, and so on. If a reporter follows this formula, the editor can cut out parts of the story because of space requirements without any difficulty. In most cases, on the Internet you are your own editor, so it's your responsibility to decide what's worth including, and what needs to be killed.

- **Use facts, and avoid fluff**. Don't waste time providing a hard sell on your company's capabilities or strengths. Stick to the facts, like the number and quality of your clients. Forget about introductory paragraphs that essentially "tell 'em what you're going to tell 'em." Leave that for your speeches. Offer readers information they can really use. And leave the public relations stuff to the public relations people.

- **Keep images to a minimum**. It's easy to add photos, graphs, charts, and other images to your work on the Internet. It's also simple to use italics, capital letters, different fonts, and boldface for emphasis. Restrain yourself, though. Too many images, or too many text highlights, will just distract your reader. The Internet is confusing enough—don't make your readers' task more difficult. On the other hand, charts and graphs do help you explain complicated points, so don't reject them out of hand.

- **Good grammar is still required**. The shorthand Twitter imposes has no place in other writing for the Internet, so be careful. You want your readers to think you are professional because you are able to express yourself professionally. Our writing refresher in chapter 3 may be worth rereading.

Add links your readers can click on. It is a great convenience, but also make sure your readers know where the links are, and not just by changing the color of the text, as Microsoft Word does when you embed a link. And if your piece is successful enough to begin a dialogue among your readers, don't just abandon what you've written. Disagreement is healthy, but if the conversation spins out of control (especially if people start hurling personal insults), it's your responsibility to gently bring the discussion back to its original path.

## Other Tips and Traps

If you're called to review someone else's writing before it is posted on the web (as many managers are), keep four things in the front of your mind. First, does the text speak to the readers you want to attract, who may know nothing about the company? What would they need to know about what you do? Second, is the information clear, concise, and above all, usable? Third, does it give readers a reason to take the action your organization wants? And fourth, are the facts correct as you understand them, and has the spelling and grammar been properly proofread?

If you're writing for an Intranet site, remember that you know your audience, so you can be a little more comfortable using acronyms and jargon. You also don't need to sell your product (although you still need to sell your argument) and you don't have to worry about getting feedback on your work—you will!

Of course, having your work read by your co-workers imposes a special obligation to write well. Get a reputation as a good writer—or simply as a good thinker—in your organization, and the sky is the limit for your career. (Of course, getting the opposite reputation can ruin your career, but follow the rules above, and you'll avoid that trap.) Be careful about being funny or flippant in your writing, even if you know everyone to whom your message is intended. Offensive jokes are career killers. Remember that it's a lot harder to discern sarcasm on the Internet than it is when you're talking to someone else. Make sure your intent is straightforward or it will be misinterpreted. And, if you can, show your work to someone else in the company you trust, and ask for that person's opinion before you post the article. A second pair of eyes is particularly useful when writing for peers and associates.

Finally, as we've said, the key to success for any written piece is the editing process. The only way to keep your writing concise, skimmable, and objective is to edit carefully and ruthlessly. If you can do that, you'll attract a loyal and faithful readership, earn the gratitude of your bosses, and unlock the full power of the Internet on your organization's behalf.

**CHAPTER 7**

# GIVE GREAT PRESENTATIONS

"There are always three speeches for every one you
actually gave. The one you practiced, the one you gave,
and the one you wish you gave."

—*Dale Carnegie*

---

### In This Chapter

- Why speeches are still important.
- Look at good and bad speech examples.
- See a sample introduction and use the checklist.
- See a systematic approach to develop and deliver
  great oral presentations.
- Check out surefire tips to make your words both
  effective and dynamic.

---

The speech—simple delivery of the spoken word to a person or group—sometimes seems like a dinosaur in the Jurassic Park of modern communication methods.

Plain old voice power is ancient when compared with digital electronic transmission of information around the world at the speed of light. And it's not just sophisticated business communication that outpaces old-fashioned speech. Today's average thirteen-year-old owns communication devices of global range and light-speed capabilities: Androids and iPhones; Blackberries and iPads; Nooks and Kindles (The Pew Research Center, 2009).

But sometimes you've just got to talk to other people. Meetings still exist (although many have gone virtual); lawyers still speak to juries; politicians still reach out to voters; and there are thousands of other occasions when the personal dimension of a face-to-face discussion, a group briefing, or a full-scale speech is just what's needed to get your point across.

Like the old grey mare, though, a speech isn't what it used to be. Our world does move faster than it used to. Newspapers have pretty much lost timeliness to television, and television, in turn, has lost its timeliness to faster, more diverse information sources like Twitter, Facebook, and Skype. People who communicate with a minimum number of keystrokes today, and make decisions with an electronic nod of the head, have little patience with wordy rambling. Consider the following scenario:

*A hush of anticipation falls over the audience as the speaker steps up to the lectern. He's tightly clutching a set of notes, suggesting he's got something important to say. Do those pages contain profound wisdom on the organization's direction? Has he solved the problem that's kept the company from joining the Fortune 500? Or at least, has he got something to say that will keep everyone entertained for a while?*

*As the air of excitement draws listeners forward on their seats to catch the speaker's opening line, his first, memorable words reverberate through the hall. "Whap…" "Whap…" "Whap…" "Is this thing on? Everyone hear me? OK, hello. Good morning, ladies and gentle-men. I'm so great to be, I mean…it's great, uh, I'm pleased to be here today."*

*(In fact, he doesn't look pleased to be there. He put his notes on top of the lectern, and now he's got a death grip on its sides.)*

*"When our program chairman, Henry Smith, called me, awhile back, and asked me to be the kickoff speaker at our annual conference, well, I was just really surprised. You know, Ol' Hank and I go back a long ways. We've been here through a number of these conferences, let me tell you. We go back to the days when our meetings were half this size, and held in the old Quonset huts—when you had to walk across the parking lot to use the Porta-Potties. Now, of course, we have this new building with the classy restrooms just inside the main entrance, but that's another story.*

*"Anyway, I was surprised this time, because it's a pretty big honor to speak at the plenary session, instead of just a breakout group, like I usually do. I should mention that I WILL also be giving my usual technical update during a couple of the breakout periods. You can find the times listed under tab seven in the back of the conference notebook.*

*But since I DO have this shot at talking to the entire group, I want to give you my take on how things are going in our field of systematic supervisory subrogation. If you'll bear with me, I've got some pretty thorough notes here, so I can give you the details concerning each of the 26 cases in adjudication."*

The speaker then reads from his thick ream of notes, not bothering to look up from the technically detailed text. It's hard to decide whether his boring reading is worse than his disconnected introduction, in which he bounced from the location of restrooms to the schedule for breakout sessions.

The excitement and energy bleeds out of the room like air from a leaking balloon. A few in the audience are still listening to the speaker just to guess, "How bad can this get?" All over the room, the dim light of smartphones can be seen, as if a swarm of fireflies had suddenly been set free. Some people are thumbing through their program notebooks, trying to figure out when they'd need to return if they staged a daring escape to their rooms, the lobby, or the golf course. Others close their eyes to concentrate and pray that they do not begin to actually snore. A lucky few who remembered to bring the *USA Today* from their room pull it out to work the crossword puzzle.

Let's trace the ugly trajectory of this presentation scenario to see where it went wrong. Our example speaker gave good indication, in those initial moments, that his presentation would be pedestrian at best. The signals said that, more than likely, it was going to be crushingly, soul-numbingly boring. Communication professors and public-speaking consultants agree that an audience forms its first impressions about a speaker in a matter of seconds. This magical time window has been cited as about seven seconds (Kinsey Goman, 2011).

Fortunately for audiences around the world, most speakers are not as bad as the person in this example. But far too many of them begin with two signal failures in those vital first few seconds: to grab the audience's attention (in a positive way, of course) and to make a good first impression. Indeed, the vast majority of public speakers waste that precious initial time with dull salutations, such as, "Good morning, I'm pleased to be here ..." or something equally vapid. Why? Our guess is that this kind of introduction does serve a perceived purpose: It calms speakers down. It gives them the opportunity to hear their voice making a somewhat reassuring—although bland—sound.

How much more compelling it would have been if the speaker in our example immediately launched into a dramatic story, made an intriguing statement of fact, or asked a provocative question! Imagine if he walked to the microphone, and began:

*Thirty-eight years ago today, a young man walked into a meeting at this very location, wearing the uniform of a U.S. Marine just released from active duty.*

*His uniform was wrinkled and smelled of mothballs from being stuffed into a sea bag—because he'd been wearing jungle utilities for a very long time. But he wore that uniform proudly anyway, especially the ribbons that reflected his service in the hardest-fought months of the Vietnam War.*

*Not everyone he'd met since returning to his country respected that uniform. Anger over the war and his country's policies had led several people to make nasty remarks as he passed by. But he'd heard there was a chance to get a job with a new organization having a meeting here—and the uniform was the only polite clothing he owned.*

*He smiled when he arrived and found that the meeting was being held in old Quonset buildings; the surplus military structures made him feel at home. When he walked in, the people at the new organization also made him feel at home. They understood the sense of patriotism that led him to wear his uniform. And they made it clear they respected his service and appreciated his sacrifices.*

*Ladies and gentlemen, I was that young marine—the guy who walked into the annual meeting of this organization, nearly four decades ago. In the years since then, I've been blessed with a good job, a lot of great co-workers, and even a few promotions along the way. I've never forgotten the way I was received here, and I've tried my best to make myself part of the accepting, supporting culture that has meant so much to me and my family. Today, I'm honored to welcome you to this plenary session of our annual meeting and to give you an update on a few key areas...*

Of course, not everyone has such a heartwarming personal story to tell. And starting off dramatically doesn't always work; sometimes a more reserved style is appropriate. But most people and most organizations have moving stories to tell, and there are lots of other ways to create a lively opening for a talk.

In our first example, the speaker compounded his poor beginning by starting to read from his notes. He didn't even try to look up every once in a while to make eye contact with his audience. This is one of public speaking's worst sins; if you treat your speech as a reading exercise, you are directly inviting your audience to tune you out and turn on their smartphones. Want to avoid this pitfall? Keep in mind that every speech, presentation, and briefing is a performance. You're not turning in a term paper or submitting a report. You're trying to make a connection with the audience.

The verbal content of a speech—the actual words people say—is not the only important thing in any presentation. Experts on spoken communication generally agree that the verbal content of a speech is less important (perhaps considerably so) than how a speaker looks and sounds. This assertion caused quite a stir at a convention for corporate speechwriters, held in Chicago a few years ago. Attendees were startled when the results of a UCLA psychology study were presented to this group of professional communicators. The study postulated there are three elements in any human communication: words, vocal sound, and the nonverbal factors of appearance and physical gestures. And it concluded, based on survey data, that audience perceptions of a speech are based 55 percent on a speaker's appearance, 33 percent on the way a speaker sounds, and only 7 percent on the actual words of the speech (Mehrabian and Wiener, 1967).

You can imagine how poorly that news was received by a group of people who write speeches for a living. But the unflappable moderator, the late journalist and spokesperson Tony Snow (who was then the press secretary for President George H.W. Bush) made several shrewd observations. First, since speechwriters chronically consider themselves to be underpaid, Mr. Snow humorously opined that everyone present might wish to keep this study confidential from their employers.

Rather than waste energy arguing which elements of public speaking are most important, Snow suggested it would be best to simply emphasize to speakers that sticking to the script is not enough: their appearance and the way they sound are extremely important.

Whether presented starkly by a social scientist, or in the understated, practical manner of Tony Snow, the message is the same: A speech is a performance. How you look and how you sound are at least as important as what you say. No matter how communication technology evolves in the future, looking and sounding prepared and professional will always be the keys to avoiding mediocrity as a speaker.

## The Design Blueprint or Outline

Every so often, you may be asked to make a unique kind of presentation, such as one that involves a skit or a song. But the majority of speeches, presentations, and even briefings consist of an introduction, a body of content (sometimes called the argument or evidence) and a conclusion.

Lots of people have different ideas on how to get your audience's attention at the beginning of a speech, but no one disagrees that it's absolutely vital to do so. Get the audience's attention immediately by making a provocative statement or telling a compelling story: something that will captivate them, pique their curiosity, or stimulate their interest.

**EXPERT TIP**

**Mary Grealy** is president of the Healthcare Leadership Council (HLC), a coalition of chief executives from several disciplines in American healthcare, including hospitals, health plans, pharmaceutical companies, medical device manufacturers, and academic health centers. Grealy gets frequent requests to provide informational briefings, congressional testimony, and other forms of public commentary. Her advice for putting together effective presentations:

- **Build your talk by collecting information about the potential audience.** This will help focus your presentation. A checklist (Figure 7.1) is a helpful tool in making sure you avoid pitfalls.
- **Find out whether audiovisuals will be appropriate and supported.** Are there any special formats or requirements?
- **Even if the meeting agenda is not final when you call, press for whatever information is available.** You can find out things to help avoid surprises.
- **When you will be part of a panel, ask who the other members will be, and the order of speakers.** Suggest that the sponsoring organization set up a conference call among panelists in advance, to avoid redundancy and to make the whole presentation more coherent.
- **Send a copy of your biography or resume to the inviting organization.** Even if they don't ask for it, it's usually appreciated. Include a short, "suggested intro" for yourself. Bring an extra copy when you go to speak (introducers sometimes don't get the advance materials, and they'll be grateful!).

Don't risk writer's block by trying to compose the exact wording of the opening during this initial outline phase. As you sketch out the rest of your presentation, and go through your research materials, you'll think of ideas for a compelling statement or moving story.

After the introduction, you may want to provide a road map, in the form of a quick preview of the things you're going to talk about. You probably don't need to do this when your talk is one in a series of panel speeches, or otherwise part of a larger presentation. But if your speech is a stand-alone presentation, the road map can help the audience follow your points more easily. Keep your preview short; spending too much time on what you intend will make the audience think you are long-winded.

The next element of your speech's blueprint is to outline the main body, or the significant points of the speech. Here's where you provide supporting ideas and details—sometimes referred to as evidence—and any examples you've developed to prove or reinforce those points. After listing the main points, the classic approach would have you provide a summary. The last item in the blueprint is the conclusion, which should project a sense of finality. So, taking a classic approach to preparing a speech outline includes

- an introduction—establishing rapport between speaker and audience

- points of evidence—presented to stimulate and convince
- a summary—succinctly recounting the argument, and carrying momentum forward
- a conclusion—wrapping up in a call to action.

---

**Figure 7.1**

A Checklist for Speeches and Presentations

Here is a list of questions to answer before you start writing your presentation:

- What organization is requesting the presentation?
- What topics are they interested in, and what other subjects should be covered?
- Where and when will the presentation be given?
- How large will the audience be, and are there any people of special importance attending?
- What are key characteristics of the audience? (If relevant, include information about their average age, education level, political orientation, and the depth of their knowledge on the subject to be discussed.)
- How much time has the inviting organization allotted for the presentation?
- What is the format of the presentation? Is it a keynote address, one in a series of presentations, or a panel discussion?
- Would the organization like to have time for questions and answers?
- What is the meeting's theme? What's the rest of the agenda like? Who else is speaking, and what are the topics of their presentations?
- Who will introduce the speaker? Who is the point of contact for the organization?
- Does the organization require a copy of the prepared remarks or a speech title in advance of the presentation? If so, when?
- What are the physical details of the presentation location, including
  - What is the stage layout?
  - How will the panel be seated?
  - How large is the lectern? (Will it accommodate my notes or a laptop; does it have a light?)
  - Will a wireless microphone be available?
  - What other audiovisual support will there be?
- What other administrative details are there, including
  - How will the speaker get to the site?
  - Who is paying the speaker's expenses?
  - Is there an honorarium? If so, how much has the organization offered?

---

## The Framework—Flesh Out the Words

Informed by the research you've done on the audience, and guided by your outline, now it's time to compose the words of the speech. Some speakers don't formally take this step. They rely on their knowledge and any outlining or notes they've prepared to allow them to speak more spontaneously.

**Figure 7.2**

Sample Introduction

On the day he was sworn in as Secretary of Veterans Affairs, Anthony Principi promised he would do his utmost to ensure that America's veterans and their families would receive all of the services and benefits they have rightfully earned from their service to our nation. It was a promise he not only kept during his four years as Secretary—but one he has kept throughout his entire life.

Secretary Principi is a proud graduate of the United States Naval Academy, was a river patrol unit commander in Vietnam, and is a former member of the Navy Judge Advocate General's Corps.

He served with distinction as chief counsel and staff director of the Senate Committee on Veterans Affairs; as counsel to the Senate Armed Services Committee; and as chair of both the Commission on Servicemembers and Veterans Transition Assistance and of President George W. Bush's Defense Base Closure and Realignment Committee. He also served three separate tours of duty with the Department of Veterans Affairs as assistant secretary, deputy secretary, and finally as VA secretary from 2001-2005.

Secretary Principi has also been the chair of the Naval Academy's Board of Visitors; the vice president for government affairs for Pfizer, and the executive chairman of QTC Management. Ladies and gentlemen, it is my privilege to introduce to you one of the greatest friends our nation's veterans have ever had: the Honorable Anthony J. Principi.

If you're going to do this, you'd better be well-versed in the subject matter, have a very orderly thought process, and be exceptionally adept at word choice. But most of us will be much better off with a little more preparation.

Even those few who speak without notes will benefit from fully constructing the framework of the speech. We recommend composing the words in advance of the presentation. The process of physically writing or typing out the words—or reading and editing drafts prepared by staff—allows you to think through arguments, find the most logical approach, and smoothly present those arguments as eloquently, briefly, and understandably as possible.

Here's another reason to write out what you're going to say, even if you don't take the words to the podium with you: The process of writing and working through the words is a proven memory aid. In many instances, speakers who have written their words in advance find they can recite long passages verbatim, with little or no reference to their notes. Then, during the actual presentation, a quick glance at talking points is all they need.

Writing for smooth expression and eloquent phrasing should not be confused with using elaborate, overly complex words and unnecessary, high-flown allusions. Especially with the spoken word, clear, simple language is the best platform for ideas and evokes the strongest feelings. This phase is also the time to comb out the acronyms, abbreviations, and techie terms that populate notes during early stages of speech building. These language shortcuts are audience losers.

## Fill in the Structure With Audience Stimulators

With a solid framework in place, fill in the structure by using techniques to emphasize important points, to make the talk lively, and to involve the audience. This includes selection of audiovisual materials, first-person stories, anecdotes, quotations, questions, and other rhetorical flourishes. Nonverbal behaviors also stimulate the audience, such as eye contact, facial expressions, posture and body orientation, proximity to the audience, and gestures.

### Audiovisuals

Audiovisual support is a key decision for a speaker today. Technology has advanced at a startling pace for digital imagery, and audience expectations and tastes have changed to follow that trend. For many people, yesterday's question, "Can I find a few illustrations for my speech?" has become today's: "Can I find a few words to accompany my illustrations?"

Desktop presentation support programs have become so capable and complex that there are many books on each program. Chapter 8 goes into more detail on which program to use and why. But videos and still images should support your presentation, not detract from it. Your goal is to find a way to deliver a successful presentation, using an effective blend of words and images.

### Rhetorical Techniques

"Rhetoric" comes from ancient Greece, where it was Aristotle's favorite subject. Rhetoric describes the way public speakers move audiences to action with arguments. And a few rhetorical techniques—like simile, analogy, and metaphor—can be useful to the average speaker.

These three figures of speech, which are sometimes confused with one another, help explain complex concepts by making comparisons to other things or ideas. The most common technique is the simile. This figure of speech describes two fundamentally different things as being similar, by using the words "like" or "as." Here are some examples:

- The speaker was as sharp as a tack.
- That unexciting presentation was like watching paint dry.

Metaphors directly describe an object or idea with a known term, implying some similarity between them. A metaphor uses one thing to mean another and creates a comparative relationship between the two words.

- The stage in front of the spotlights was an oven.
- The moderator was boiling mad when my speech ran overtime.

An analogy is a comparison of certain similarities between things which are otherwise unlike:

- Writing a speech without an outline has much in common with planning a voyage without a chart.

- Giving an important speech without rehearsing your lines is the kind of gamble you take when playing an important sports game without having practiced.

The key to using rhetorical techniques is to make your points clear by putting life into your words.

## Quotations

Famous quotations are as integral to public speaking as the lectern or podium at the front of the hall. In pre-Internet days, the bookshelves of any self-respecting speechwriter, as well as those of many executives, prominently featured *Bartlett's Familiar Quotations*. After all, what better way to imply the profound nature of a speaker's observations than to express them through a proverb, or the words of a famous person? The strategy can be effective. Audiences traditionally have a reverence for wisdom or humor so aptly expressed that the words have stood the test of time. And there's no shortage of material. Among the most prolifically quoted are sources so famous that only one name need be cited: Shakespeare, Franklin, Lincoln, Thoreau, Emerson, Churchill. With today's Internet search engines and old-fashioned texts filled with famous quotations, you can find an insightful or witty saying to open any talk, support any argument, and evocatively put a period at the end of any conclusion.

To make effective use of quotations, choose wisely and sparingly. Audiences may enjoy reflecting on a quote from antiquity, or from a prominent, quirky celebrity—perhaps Yogi Berra—if the saying fits the situation that's being discussed or the point that's being made. But when it's hard to relate the quote to the subject at hand, or when the speaker uses too many quotes, it's no longer a beneficial tactic.

Among professional speechwriters working in politics, there is a near-insatiable demand for quotes extolling our nation's virtues. Inevitably, the search leads virtually all of them to one particular source: Alexis de Tocqueville (de Tocqueville, 1835). As the noble experiment of democracy was born, few individuals wrote more expansively or glowingly about the majesty of America and its democratic virtues than this French observer; his fulsome words have become so overused among contemporary speechwriters that a standing joke among political scribes is, "Don't quote de Tocque."

Here's some bottom-line summary advice for using quotes: Keep it on point, keep it limited, and keep it fresh. As Mark Twain advised: "Everything has its limit; iron ore cannot be educated into gold."

## The Rule of Threes

One of the most powerful techniques for bringing your words to life, as well as one of the easiest to build into your presentation, is the rule of threes. The term "rule of threes" has application in math, medicine, music, and architecture. But it is best known as a technique applied to writing and public speaking. From the earliest examples of literature (Julius Caesar's line, "Veni, Vidi, Vici"—I came, I saw, I conquered—is one of the first that has survived), writers have exhibited an understanding of the power of three.

There is a sweeping influence of the rule of threes in our language. It is a prevalent plot structure in fables, stories, and jokes. The rule of threes is found everywhere:

- religious writings (Father, Son, and Holy Spirit)
- scientific classifications (animal, vegetable, mineral)
- articulation of public policy (of the people, by the people, for the people)
- religious virtues (faith, hope, and charity)
- descriptions of what's important in our society (life, liberty, and the pursuit of happiness)
- memorable book and movie titles (*The Good, the Bad, and the Ugly* and *Sex, Lies, and Videotape*).

Listening to a speech subjects us to a flow of thoughts and ideas, challenging us to somehow organize this new information. The offer of three clearly identified points within this flow appeals to our sense of order; we're given some handholds to help us grip the meaning of the speaker's words. The rule of threes is also helpful for making gestures. Ticking off three points on your fingers is a natural way of using your hands. Any time you can articulate three points in your speech with effusive but graceful hand gestures, you will bring a sense of order to your argument in a lively way.

In writing your presentation, you may be fortunate enough to identify naturally occurring sets of three. But successful writers and speakers also find ways to create them. For example, Shakespeare wanted to write more compelling words to start Mark Antony's eulogy for Caesar than: "My friends," or "My fellow Romans." He could describe the audience as friends, and they were also Romans. Could he find a third way to describe them? How much more powerful it was to say "Friends, Romans, countrymen, lend me your ears."

In a more contemporary example, imagine a politician who wants to tell an audience that a new interstate road proposal will be good for commuters, and—because it's cost effective—also good for taxpayers. How could this speaker add another beneficiary, to facilitate the rule of threes? How about: "This proposal is good for commuters; it's good for taxpayers; it's good for America!"

If your presentation involves more than three points, strongly consider citing only three. Let's say, for instance, there are 11 challenges facing your organization, or that your division has recorded nine accomplishments. A good approach is to mention the actual number, and then call attention to just three examples. You will use the power of threes, but you'll also recognize the reality that most audiences can't assimilate a long list of points presented orally.

As useful as the rule of threes may be, it shouldn't be applied rigidly; there are instances in which two, or four, or some other number of points is so important that they shouldn't be artificially changed. Patrick Henry's famous statement included two parts that would not be improved by the addition of a third: "Give me liberty, or give me death."

## Dress, Body Language, Stage Kinetics, and Paralinguistics

As discussed earlier, audience perception of a speaker depends on how the speaker looks and sounds. Appearance begins with attire—a significant factor in business communication. For the days you need to give a speech or major presentation, here are some tips.

Dark gray and dark blue suits (or sport jacket/slacks combos) are the safest bets for both men and women. White shirts and blouses may not sound exciting or fashionable, but in a hotel meeting room they're your best bet to accent a business suit, especially when seen from the back of the room. Keep your suit jacket buttoned during your presentation and you'll automatically look more businesslike. Wear it open, and you'll have a more casual look. One is not better than the other, yet you make a statement about attitude toward subject matter and audience with the option you choose.

Personal accessories, including jewelry and wristwatches, can distract your listeners if they dominate your visual presentation. If you are not sure about how your accessories will affect your audience, keep them in your pocket or briefcase until after the presentation. Avoid tinted glasses, which tend to block eye contact.

### Body Language

Body language includes posture, gestures, facial expressions, and eye movement. The physical posture of a speaker is a matter of personal preference, but you should follow a few general principles. Except for situations involving humor or other theatrical productions, speakers should have a professional appearance, one that's attentive and respectful of the audience. It's OK for a speaker to appear relaxed, but this should not extend to leaning on the podium or slouching.

Gestures and facial expressions should be vigorously used to bring a speaker's words to life. Expressive people who naturally use their hands while telling a story should do the same while giving a speech or presentation. You should also change your facial expressions to show feelings toward your words.

If you don't habitually use your hands expressively while talking, you should work on making gestures during a speech. Introverted speakers can start by adding a few gestures, perhaps with directional phrases ("the facility moved way out west" while sweeping an arm out to indicate direction), or phrases with size ("caught a very small fish," demonstrating by holding up your hand, showing your thumb close to your forefinger). Remember, it's easy and appears natural for most speakers to tick off three points on their fingers.

Since a presentation is typically given in front of a larger audience, and the speaker may be a bit constricted by standing behind a lectern, it's usually necessary for speakers to make their gestures more energetic. We've given many presentation training classes. We videotape student presentations, asking them to make their gestures more dramatic. We encourage them to really "push it out" during their talk. When our students watch the video, they are surprised to see the gestures that felt overdone look just about right at the lectern.

Eye gaze is important. It's not hard to control your eye movement during a presentation. It's a technique, however, often neglected due to the distractions of reading text, using audiovisual aids, and the pressure of being onstage. Looking at members of the audience immediately shows them the speaker is attentive to them. Once they see this, audience members think it's polite to devote their attention in return to the speaker. Depending on the physical layout of the site, most speakers will need to move and change eye gaze direction in an organized way to engage the audience in all areas of the room.

It's not necessary for the speaker to look directly into the eyes of individual members of the audience. Looking at a particular area of the room will have a halo effect of making a dozen people in that area believe they are the ones singled out by the speaker.

It's important to not change your eye gaze so quickly that you appear shifty-eyed. If a speaker's eye gaze only lingers in an area for a second or two at a time before moving rapidly away, the audience will get the impression of insincerity. Sustain your eye gaze to a particular area for 20 seconds or more before moving on to another area of the room.

## Stage Kinetics

Stage kinetics—the speaker's movement around the room—also has visual impact. In the performing arts, this is a subject of careful study. Actors, dancers, and singers all move around the stage with purpose. Performers comfortable with the stage—such as comedians and motivational speakers—also use movement to add theatrical flair, change the mood of a discussion, and highlight changed emotion in their voice. Done well, the movement adds to the performance. The risk is that the movement will seem artificial, look awkward, and serve as a distraction.

Some managers recoil at the thought of moving around the stage; they fear coming out from behind the cover of the lectern. It's understandable to feel nervous about leaving the lectern's perceived comfort zone, but it offers a big payoff. Getting away from the lectern brings you closer to your audience.

In some oral presentation situations—like a Bible reading in a church service—it's most appropriate to stand behind a lectern. But for other speaking situations, we strongly advise you to create your own space, by standing to one side of the lectern. This will put you more in touch with your audience and will facilitate more natural hand and arm gestures.

Before you decide whether it's appropriate to move away from the lectern, you should consider the room's acoustics. If you're in a small room and no voice amplification is required, the problem is solved; the audience will hear you as well or better away from any lectern. If a system of microphones and speakers is in use, and the meeting has on-site audiovisual support, ask in advance for a wireless microphone. This is a common request, and most audiovisual techs will have lavalier microphones for this purpose. Lavalier microphones clip onto a necktie, coat lapel, or shirt collar.

For most presenters, just standing next to the lectern, gesturing naturally, and using the other effective body language techniques will provide the audience with plenty of visual stimulation. But speakers can add dimension, reinforce a point, and add a sense of urgency by moving just a small distance.

In order to make a strong point, you can begin a statement, pause, and then take two or three purposeful steps forward, stop, and deliver the rest of your decisive line. Then, after speaking for a bit, you can retreat to your starting point.

In most cases, there's not much to be gained from further movement around the stage, and it's definitely a bad idea to wander aimlessly around the room while you speak. A few speakers like to walk completely around the room, like grade school teachers watching students for misbehavior; most experts agree this is distracting and unsettling to the audience.

One sin of stage kinetics is leaning from side to side, or rocking in place. Some speakers hope this swaying motion expresses dynamic feeling, but it does not. Audiences invariably comment negatively on the "rockers," saying such purposeless movement is distracting.

## Paralinguistics

A number of nonverbal factors contribute to the way a speaker sounds, and include the tone, pitch, rhythm, volume, and inflection. With a little thought and planning, most speakers can vary these attributes. This makes a tremendous difference in bringing their words to life.

The easiest way to work out effective uses of these vocal techniques is by rehearsing your presentation. As you practice saying your lines aloud in varying tempos, changing the timing of pauses, tone, and inflections, you will discover many new ways to give your words meaning and impact.

## Use of Humor

For a long time after World War II, from the 1950s to the mid-1990s, speakers started off their presentations with a joke or two, before getting into the serious substance of their speech. Professional speechwriters of the era needed a hefty joke file and a few fresh stories every week to keep up with the demand for humor.

Humor in public speaking is still alive and well, but the routine in which speakers told two full traditional jokes—with setups and punch lines—has become passé.

Today's effective speakers still recognize the value of humor as an icebreaker, putting the audience at ease, and establishing a friendly rapport. But instead of contrived jokes, they typically try to comment on something funny related to the subject matter or event.

Aside from the question of how to inject humor into your speech, ask yourself: Should you? There is a clear downside. What if no one laughs? Some experts, like well-known speaking coach Nick Morgan, say using humor is definitely not for everyone. "Humor is hazardous to the health of public speakers. You've got to do humor well or it falls flat— and that's worse than no humor at all (Morgan, 2009)."

Yet humor can make you likable, put the audience at ease, and bring your words to life in an entertaining way. Using humor can be risky, but if it is done in a way relatable to the audience or event, it's worth it.

For most speakers, the best way to add humor is to tell an anecdote or funny story about something that happened to them personally, or to someone around them. Humorous incidents from everyday life are easy to relate, and they come across as genuine. Self-effacing humor can be an especially powerful tool. It's easy, and effectively shows the audience you don't take yourself too seriously.

Edward J. Derwinski, who became the first Secretary of Veterans Affairs when the Veterans Administration was elevated to a Cabinet Department, had a signature technique in self-denigrating humor. During his frequent speeches to veterans organizations, he made sure his introduction included the fact that he had been a private in the army. Then, stepping to the lectern, Derwinski said he needed to correct the impression that he had not been able to gain superior rank during his service all through World War II: "Because of my instinctive leadership qualities, my command of military situations, and my ability to lead, when I left the army, I was a corporal." This always brought a big laugh, and warmed the audience toward him.

You should keep a joke file. But instead of outmoded jokes, fill your file with notes on amusing things that happen to you, cartoons that depict funny ways to look at your field of work, and other humorous contrasts from your observations and experience. This kind of humor may not get the audience rolling on the floor laughing, but it may provide the right touch to bring your words to life in a comfortable way.

## Stage Fright

Remember Speech 101? Some of you will never forget the symptoms that built as you waited to give your talk in front of the class: your hands would sweat, your mouth would go dry, your knees trembled, and there was an uncontrollable blush spreading over your neck and face. You wanted to control those things, but they were a low priority compared with worries about your racing heart rate and butterflies in your stomach.

Fear hung in the air like diesel fumes as you approached the lectern. You looked to your fellow students for reassurance, but you didn't get much eye contact from others in speech class. Your classmates who were going to speak after you were busy rehearsing their lines in silent fear; those who had finished were slumped down, too relieved their ordeal was over to care.

Performance anxiety is a well-documented phobia, fueled by powerful chemical reactions in the body. Fear of speaking in public triggers the release of a substantial dose of adrenaline into the bloodstream, and the symptoms—reflecting the body's preparation for human fight-or-flight behavior—naturally follow.

Contrary to the way many speakers feel, people don't die from stage fright. Even if some speakers have serious heart issues, they don't die from being on stage. Stage fright won't kill you, but it might kill your chances of giving a good presentation. There are ways to reduce this huge, fearful situation to a more manageable size. First, consider who's affected by it and why, and then identify ways to counteract it.

Speech coaches like to point out that a majority of people list public speaking among their greatest fears—ahead of insects, heights, flying, and even death. It's fun for experts to say: "It appears people really mean it when they say they'd rather die than give a speech."

So stage fright is universal. Fear of speaking in public is not an individual affliction. It's a normal feeling, common to everyone who steps up to the lectern. Even professional entertainers feel the effects of this natural process—some quite strongly. But because they recognize the symptoms for what they are, the pros press on, using these feelings to stimulate more energy in their performance.

To confront stage fright, ask: "What am I afraid of?" It could be failure, rejection, looking foolish, or fear of the unknown. None of these are trivial matters or impossible outcomes. A speaker could definitely look foolish. But with proper preparation and a reasonable appraisal of the situation, you can be confident those fears will not be realized, and your presentation will result in a good experience. Stage fright is initially invisible to the audience. While you may feel your fear is obvious, the audience is not reading the symptoms. At least, the audience doesn't see the nervousness, unless the speaker announces the affliction, either in his own words, or by exhibiting one or more "stage fright giveaways."

A speaker might say, "I guess you can tell I'm a bit nervous," hoping to win either acceptance or sympathy from the audience. Unfortunately, this has the opposite effect, and causes discomfort among the audience as they then focus on the slightest mannerisms, looking for telltale signs of weakness. Nonverbal giveaways include holding onto the sides of the lectern in a rigid grip, jingling change in your pocket, wringing your hands together, and rapidly shifting your weight from foot to foot. Knowledgeable speakers can avoid these telltale signs, and not look like they have stage fright. But is it possible for them not to *feel* like they have it?

## Rehearsal—the Fine-Tune Phase

It's a great idea to practice your talk with a stopwatch. Once you see how the timing works, you will need to edit your material to make the talk fit the allotted time, speaking at your normal pace. As you see how long it takes to give your presentation, make timing marks in your notes, highlighted in color. These navigation marks can include the half-way mark, a minute to go, and any other signals to yourself that might add to your comfort level.

When you actually give the speech, you'll probably find your pace varies a bit from your rehearsal. But the practice should get you very close to the actual timing. If you can rehearse in front of a captive audience such as friends and family, you'll make your practice timing even more accurate. While rehearsing, indulge your natural inclination to emphasize points with gestures, facial expressions, and changes in vocal inflection. If you plan to use props or references while on the stage, practice moving them into place in a smooth fashion. If you're planning to use audiovisuals that will require slide changes, practice using a remote without feeling constricted by it. Either put it down on the lectern, or hold it in an unobtrusive manner.

**EXPERT TIP**

For a dozen years, clinical psychologist **Dana L. Moore**, PhD, studied the effects of stage fright on speakers in an executive development program. After many counseling sessions with participants, she recommends these steps to deal with speaker anxiety.

- **Prepare for the event, to remove or reduce the element of the unknown**. This includes knowing as much as possible about the event and the audience. Thoroughly master your presentation material, including the sequence and timing.

- **If possible, visit the site of the speech before the event**, and walk through the approach to the lectern to get a feel for the physical location. This familiarity will banish many unknowns.

- **Memorize the first line of the presentation**. "Being able to reliably deliver that first line is an important security blanket," she says.

- **Establish a relaxation procedure for yourself**. Try a routine like the following, a short time before getting up to speak:

  - Take a few deep breaths.

  - Visualize a calming scene, like lying on a beach or walking through a quiet forest.

  - Slowly say "relax" to yourself.

## Put It All Together—the Speech

It's time to give your presentation. Walk up to the lectern, place your notes on top, and pause to look at the audience. Unless this is a very somber occasion—a eulogy—you should smile. The pause has a powerful effect of establishing your command of the situation. It will also calm your nerves. Don't bail out by giving a salutation or making a comment on the previous speaker. Use the compelling opening you've written, starting with your memorized first line.

As you develop your theme, move away from the lectern; stand next to it or within a couple feet. Remember to work the whole room with your eye gaze, and take the opportunities— which you discovered while rehearsing—to gesture naturally. Be enthusiastic as you warm to your subject, and use the facial expressions and changes in the vocal tone you anticipated earlier.

Keep track of time, making use of the marks you put in your notes during rehearsal. If you can, have a co-worker signal you from the back of the room when the time allotted your presentation is almost done. As you wind up your talk using that nice concluding line you wrote, stand silent for a few seconds at the lectern before walking away. It will be your time to enjoy the recognition of the audience for a great presentation!

**CHAPTER 8**

# USE POWERPOINT OR NOT

"My belief is that PowerPoint doesn't kill meetings.
People kill meetings."

*—Peter Norvig, Director of Research, Google Inc.*

### In This Chapter

- Will visuals add anything to the presentation?
- Why is there a myth that PowerPoint leads to boring presentations?
- See the differences between a few bad PowerPoint presentations.
- Why you should still use PowerPoint.
- The default path to effective PowerPoint presentations.

Stories about presentation snafus are common, but here's one that focuses on what an amazing tool we have in today's computer-generated audiovisuals: In the early 1990s, a public-speaking coach was invited to present to nearly 500 senior federal managers on the West Coast, at a meeting held at a navy facility on Treasure Island in San Francisco.

He prepared an hour-long presentation, which had fairly complex items: instructional charts and graphs, photographic images on slides, and six short videos. He had no computer-generated graphics at the time. A fledgling version of PowerPoint for Macintosh had been available for a few years, but it was not widely used and it had limited capabilities. So his carry-on luggage was a large duffle bag with a box of letter-sized Viewgraphs (transparency film pages with cardboard frames), a tray of 35 mm slides, and a pile of half-inch videotapes.

He arrived at the auditorium before the event, scrambling to test out and adjust the overhead projector (requiring clumsy hand movements for each transparency). The

Kodak carousel-type slide projector also needed setup to run smoothly, and his videos needed to be cued up on the VCR player. Switching from the live parts of his presentation to the audiovisual elements was not going to be seamless.

After some amusing last-minute antics to temporarily repair a VCR, and some on-the-fly editing to remove references to slides jammed in the carousel, he survived the event. But the contrast between those multimedia techniques of less than two decades ago with the current generation of sophisticated graphics presentation tools is surprisingly large. It's like comparing the Wright Flyer with an F-18 Super Hornet.

Wilbur and Orville invented their own rules for their simple flights, but the pilot of the F-18 needs instruction and training before climbing into the cockpit. Similarly, users of modern computer-generated graphics can benefit from instruction before grabbing the controls.

## How to Use Audiovisuals in Your Presentation

The first challenge is whether you need to use audiovisual aids at all. Ask yourself—and give it careful thought—will audiovisuals add anything to this particular presentation?

Virtually every expert on presentations will tell you that visuals should *only* be used to enhance a speech, not to take its place. *You* must be the star of your presentation; slides, videos, and any other audiovisuals can *only* be used in a supporting role.

Used correctly, computer-generated visuals can make a good presentation great. Used incorrectly, they can make that same good presentation terrible. In part of this chapter, we'll show several ways audiovisuals can detract from a speech.

In deciding whether to use audiovisuals, think about the size of the audience and the length of the presentation. For a very short presentation to a small group, fooling around with slides might get in the way of making a connection with your audience.

In such situations, don't underestimate old-fashioned flipcharts and chalkboards. They may lack modern panache, but they have the powerful advantage of allowing you to be dynamic in working with them. They also lend themselves to interaction with the audience (by writing question marks, drawing connecting lines between subjects on the board, and so on).

In small group settings, consider holding up a relevant photo, chart, or book. With photos and charts, it's effective to enlarge them and mount them on chipboard. Such items serve as props—giving you something to physically display and gesture toward. These are proven ways to animate your posture before the audience, which will put life in your talk. But you should know about more sophisticated audiovisuals, especially through computer generation. Then you can make the best decision for your specific presentation.

First, there are many names for computer-generated presentation aids: audiovisuals, A/Vs, computer-generated graphics, slides, visual aids, presentation software, and so on. We refer to it all together under the term "PowerPoint."

Several programs are available for computer generation of presentation visuals, but PowerPoint is the software likely to be found in the audiovisual support equipment in most conference rooms and meeting locations. PowerPoint can also open and do a basic conversion of presentations prepared in many other software applications.

If you work at a large firm that has a presentational graphic design specialist on staff, keep that person's number handy in your office contacts list. If you do have an expert to call on, this chapter will help focus your needs for high quality graphics in discussions with that specialist. If you don't have the luxury of an expert on staff, this chapter will help lead you along a path to produce effective graphic materials.

With PowerPoint it's easier to see what you should do by looking at what you shouldn't do. So we'll examine a couple examples of typical PowerPoint abuse—one by a neophyte user and one by a more experienced presenter. Identifying the pitfalls in these two presentation disasters will allow us to develop contrasting charts of Dos and Don'ts. (See Figures 8.1 and 8.2.)

**Figure 8.1**

Neophyte Dos and Don'ts

**Don't:**

- Use brightly colored backgrounds—it's hard to see the text.
- Have insufficient contrast between colors of background and other elements.
- Have a complex background—it's hard to differentiate content.
- Use many colors in no particular order—this shows a lack of continuity.
- Have small text and images—they will look unimpressive.
- Use many fonts haphazardly—some bold, italic, underlined, in inconsistent manner.
- Use fonts that are incompatible.
- Use varied, drawn out, and overdone transitions.
- Have extensive, wild animation that seems pointless and distracting.
- Have unwarranted sound effects—it adds to the frivolous impression.

**Do:**

- Use a subdued background (allows text to stand out).
- Have high contrast between background and text, makes messages sharp.
- Use a simplified background (makes simple content more compelling).
- Use few, compatible colors with consistency, promotes sense of continuity.
- Enlarge text and images to enhance impact.
- Restrict fonts to two, and use in a consistent way.
- Make sure the fonts are compatible.
- Have quick, subtle transitions.
- Limit the use of animation—it preserves professionalism.
- Abstain from sound effects, unless they are for a specific purpose.

**Figure 8.2**

Lazy Presenter Dos and Don'ts

**Don't:**

- Put your entire presentation on slides.
- Use complete sentences.
- Put too much text per slide.
- Mindlessly convert all your speech sentences to bullets.
- Run long sequences of bullet slides that look alike.
- Add lots of elements and labels when using charts and tables, in order to make your illustrations as complex and imposing as possible.

**Do:**

- Use shorthand words on slides; add text to clarify and expound in notes section.
- Use only key words on slides.
- Use only a few words per slide.
- Try to reduce use of bullets, replacing them with definitions, artwork, tables, and charts.
- Break up parade of bullets with a different-looking slide every four or five slides.
- Simplify the number of elements in charts and tables to promote faster comprehension.

We won't provide a click-by-click guide for manipulating various versions of the PowerPoint application. All versions of PowerPoint offer a powerful, searchable help feature. If you want textual guidance on the minutiae to accomplish specific tasks, the *For Dummies* books are excellent. Get the one specific to your release of PowerPoint.

There are many features in PowerPoint, and we suggest ways to reduce the number of decisions a busy manager has to make to create a simple, but solidly professional presentation. The end of the chapter will feature a basic default settings path that the nondesign expert can use to put together an effective presentation quickly.

## Dilbert, on "Entering the PowerPoint Zone"

In spite of the quality of the visuals it can produce and its user friendliness, PowerPoint attracts a startling amount of criticism. The idea that PowerPoint leads to boring presentations has become so widespread the *Dilbert* comic picked up the story line. In one strip, a co-worker says to Dilbert, "I hope you won't mind my pillow and blanket at your presentation today." In the next frame, the co-worker explains, "The last time you presented, I lost consciousness and broke my nose on the table." In the real world, let's consider a typical office scenario that probably reflects a situation most of us have personally observed.

## PowerPoint Trauma Via the New User

*This is it, the first weekly staff meeting at Tru-Glow Energy at which everyone has to give a short presentation on the status of their program. The boss thinks this is a good way for everyone to keep up to date, while gaining useful presenting skills. Among the staff of inexperienced speakers, a lack of enthusiasm is an understatement.*

*Except for Henry. You mention to a workmate the suspiciously eager way Henry volunteered to go first to present, and learn that ol' Hank has just taught himself how to use PowerPoint. He's been raving about how he "learned the program in only 15 minutes," and has been bragging about impressing the boss. So when Henry struts up to take over the podium from the boss, you're expecting a glitzy, high-class slide show, requiring your grudging applause, as Henry makes everyone else look bad by comparison.*

*Henry puffs out his chest and begins in a loud voice, "You lucky people have the good fortune today to see our very first PowerPoint show; and even better, it's about the most exciting and productive division of Tru-Glow Energy—the Micro Wind Turbine Section!" You stifle a sneer as you wait for the first slide, which you've always heard should grab attention. It does—in shockingly garish fashion. From the conference room's speakers come the sounds of rockets launching as the darkened flat screen illuminates a bright purple background. Then multi-colored text begins to appear, as if the letters are being sequentially typed onto the screen. After several seconds of this circus-like transition, the image is complete: three varied fonts spell out "Micro Wind Turbine" in a riot of different colors. You quickly glance around the room; several people look surprised, and some exchange looks that seem to ask if this is a joke. An undismayed, beaming Henry clicks the remote.*

*The screen changes to a sickly chartreuse background, and the sound of screeching car brakes emanates from the speakers, as bright yellow text skids onto the screen to spell out "Awesome progress this quarter." Before queasy stomachs can settle from the off-putting blend of colors, the gaudy text suddenly shatters to the sound effect of a loud car crash, and a new line of bright red text spirals around the screen, finally halting in place to say "Breaking company records." This time the audience reaction is a mix of grimaces, shaking heads, and eyes squinted shut. But the audience is captive, which you realize is the particular hell of PowerPoint gone bad.*

*This presentation is bad and getting worse, as Henry announces, "I'll now flesh out my report by describing my 68 accomplishments this quarter. To save time, I've been able to squeeze eight or nine of these cool bullets on each slide." A rambling parade of text-jammed slides, in ever shifting fonts and colors, flies on and off continuously changing backgrounds, suggesting Henry's determination to try every possible variation. More annoying sound effects contribute to the growing consensus that this presentation is establishing some important benchmark for imaginative bad taste.*

*It seems an eternity, but the presentation finally screeches to an end. Henry's dreadful show made an impression that kept people talking for days about which parts of the presentation they hated most.*

What they'd just suffered reflected what veteran presentation guru Rick Altman calls "The 15 Minutes Syndrome." People who have learned just a few basic operations of PowerPoint are inclined to become hyper-excited about the powerful tools in the application. In his witty and insightful book, *Why Most PowerPoint Presentations Suck and How You Can Make Them Better*, Altman says too many brash novices like Henry rush into presentations without understanding nuances such as properly contrasting colors, appropriate size and compatibility of fonts, and the need to limit text per slide. Altman cites another phenomenon which may explain why presenters use annoying sound effects and overly dramatic animation. They're driven to "use a feature based on recency of discovery, rather than appropriateness to the task. You use it because you just learned it!"

# PowerPoint Trauma Via the Veteran—But Lazy—User

*Back at Tru-Glow Energy, there is another weekly staff meeting. The boss had cancelled those status reports for a while, understandably fearing a repeat of Henry's fiasco with PowerPoint. Now some time has passed, and a number of people on the staff have learned to use PowerPoint reasonably well. That training class the boss scheduled helped a lot, getting the message across about avoiding the horrors perpetrated by Henry.*

*Today is Betty's turn to shine—or not—with PowerPoint. Betty's at the other end of the spectrum from Henry: not at all enthusiastic about speaking. In fact, she says that's why she particularly appreciates PowerPoint, because all she had to do was just copy the main points of her regular status reports into the outline part of the program, and it automatically typed all the text out on her slides.*

*Betty looks like a distinguished presenter as she walks to the conference room's lectern. Her conservative attire and professional appearance give promise that her presentation will be interesting. As the boss reminds everyone this is the second in a series of section status reports, she picks up the remote slide changer, clicks the equipment to life, and begins.*

*"Colleagues, I'm pleased to be here today, to provide you with the latest information on the most important division here at Tru-Glow: solar panel generation. I know all of you think your own divisions have important challenges, concerning things like the new dimensions of the grid, mixed generation, microgeneration and all the other technological options. Yet, when you consider the action in my area: economic benefits, environmental aspects, and political impact—not to mention the sheer beauty of solar photovoltaic panels, which far exceed the capabilities of puny micro wind turbines and filthy subsoil extractors—it's pretty clear my division is where the action is.*

*Fortunately for you, I've created a very comprehensive PowerPoint presentation that addresses all these matters and more, including all the minutiae. This is quite an extensive A/V show, so we'll need to move pretty rapidly in order to get through these several dozen slides in the next hour. So I ask everyone to hold their questions until the end.*

*I've actually spelled out my presentation word-for-word on these slides, so I'm confident that you'll find all the answers in the following bullet points. If there's time available at the end, I'll try to answer your unusual questions."*

*Betty continues at a rapid pace, reading all of the text on each slide before clicking to the next, and the next, and the next...as a familiar blue-hued light floats out through the room, reflected on the silent, unseeing eyes. It quickly becomes apparent that this blue-hued ocean of information is sweeping past the audience, gaining little interest and less assimilation.*

## The PowerPoint Pain Index

It would be tough to determine which of the two Tru-Glow presentations was more annoying. Henry's use of irrelevant sound effects and superfluous animation—along with other inept elements—seemed pretty extreme. But according to surveys of average audiences, Betty might take the honors. Of all the facets of boredom and irritation imposed on audiences in PowerPoint presentations, the item cited as most annoying is when the speaker reads the slides word-for-word.

**EXPERT TIP**

**Dave Paradi,** author of *The Visual Slide Revolution*, conducted surveys in 2003, 2005, and 2010, gauging audience reaction to PowerPoint presentations. "The survey results point to the need for presenters to increase the use of relevant visuals to replace text and allow more of a conversation with the audience instead of a recitation of the slide text." Among Paradi's findings:

- **The top-ranked most-annoying thing about PowerPoint** was the same in each survey: "The speaker read the slides to us."

- **Another consistent complaint** was that "slides contained full sentences instead of bullet points."

- **People were annoyed by** "text on slides so small I couldn't read it," as well as by distracting, gratuitous use of animation.

Author Dave Paradi reports on his surveys in his blog, and the info on the latest is at *http://www.thinkoutsidetheslide.com/articles/annoying_powerpoint_survey_2011.htm*.

## Don't Be Scared Off—the Case for PowerPoint

With all these warnings, horror stories, complaints, and criticisms concerning PowerPoint, why would anyone bother? Poorly done PowerPoint may be awful, but when it's done right, it looks and feels good. That's not very scientific, but everyone who's seen a well-done presentation with high quality digital imagery and good complementary music knows the effect is almost magical. When properly designed and used correctly by a capable presenter, it seems obvious that the additional visual dimension gains audience attention and helps to convey the message.

And beyond such feel-good observations, there is solid, scientific proof of the value of adding audiovisual support. Researchers at the University of California, Santa Barbara, found that the human mind uses two pathways to receive information: One processes verbal information, and the other processes visual. When both types of information are received simultaneously, comprehension is significantly higher than in instances where only one pathway is used (Mayer and Moreno, 2005).

Interestingly, the same study concluded that words are better presented audibly than visually. In this research, students who listened to words in a narration scored far higher in comprehension of the material than students who simply saw the same words in onscreen text. This reinforces advice provided elsewhere in this chapter to limit text on slides, in favor of presenting the information verbally.

## The Default Path to Effective PowerPoint

So you've thought it over carefully, decided to add PowerPoint to your presentation, and you've taken note of the "dos" and "don'ts" suggested by the problematic presentations described earlier. Now it's time to help you quickly put together an effective presentation by using some of the PowerPoint program's best default settings, and taking a few other shortcuts.

The gang at Tru-Glow suffered so much in helping us see the pitfalls, it seems only fair to let them see the brighter side of the program. So let's imagine the boss hasn't given up yet. This time, he calls on Gary to provide a status report on his division in the company.

Gary's not much of an artistic type, and he has only a basic acquaintance with PowerPoint. But he did suffer through the previous two presentations at Tru-Glow staff meetings. His initial move is to check his notes to make sure he doesn't repeat the mistakes Henry and Betty made in their PowerPoint train wrecks. Then Gary comes up with a three-step game plan to survive this presentation.

First, he'll compose the textual part of his remarks, because he knows PowerPoint is just a visual tool to aid the words he'll speak. As he does his writing, he'll try to think of a couple charts, graphs, or photos he might use to help illustrate his points. He'll start with a simple outline, then type out his remarks either word-for-word or abbreviated.

In Gary's second step, he'll fire up the PowerPoint program, and look for a ready-made presentation template. Anytime you create a new presentation, you have the choice of starting with a blank presentation, or a template prepared by design specialists. Unless you're a professional designer, or someone with an artistic flair along with a good grasp of color coordination and font compatibility, go with the predesigned template. Some organizations and conference planners create a standard template that they ask all presenters to use for consistency and to reinforce the theme of a particular meeting. Gary's counting on this approach to set his presentation up with attractive, complementary colors, compatible type fonts, properly sized text, and maybe even to suggest a logical sequencing of his points.

In step number three, Gary will break down his presentation into individual thoughts or points—each of which will be the subject of a single slide. Some of those slides may contain a small number of sub points (bullets); others may present a table or photograph. His outline will guide him in segmenting the talk into the necessary bite-sized portions of text. As he creates the individual slides, Gary will paste the relevant portions of full text from his written remarks into the Notes area of PowerPoint. He will print these out later, and use them as his script during projection of the slides.

In the few minutes Gary spent standing in the back of a PowerPoint class, he heard that using an off-the-shelf template doesn't mean there's no room for creativity, or that you don't need to exercise good judgment. The instructor pointed out that not all templates are perfect—or even usable—just because professionals created them. She also said that a lot of them have pretty images, but are useless for a business presentation because of overly complex backgrounds.

But Gary is confident he'll find a good choice in the 50 or so templates and themes preloaded in the latest version of PowerPoint. To decrease the chance someone in the audience already might have seen the slide background he selects—making it seem his presentation lacks freshness—Gary could select a template from Microsoft's free online library. PowerPoint's *Available Templates and Themes* menu offers the option to search online for Office.com templates.

If your computer has an Internet connection, you can choose *PowerPoint Presentations and Slides* from the *File*, then *New* menus, and you're taken seamlessly to several categories of templates, from academic presentations to training. The business category, just one category in this group, offers more than 100 templates.

You can also do a generic search of the web for templates and themes, many of which are advertised as free, but beware—clicking on some of these freebies prompts the donating website to aim cookies and adware at your computer.

## Follow the Double-Click Road: Exact Steps to a Good Default Presentation

Gary opens up the PowerPoint program, clicks *File*, then *New*. The screen shows *Available Templates and Themes*. He scrolls across three items and clicks on *Sample Templates*.

The next menu brings up several choices, including one that catches Gary's eye: *Project Status Report*. When he double clicks on this icon, the template loads into his computer. The template automatically opens in the *Home* tab, and Gary is presented with an attractive title slide, and a selection of 10 more complementary slides with varied formats to allow presentation of information in conventional bullet style, flow charts, and timelines.

At this point, Gary is ready to input his text and other information directly onto the slides. He will do this one slide at a time, highlighting the placeholder text, and then typing in the points he already prepared on his outline. For starters, he finds that one placeholder on the title page doesn't have to be changed, so he decides to keep the text: "Project Status Report."

But then he needs to add some new text, and there's not another placeholder. No problem. On the *Insert* tab, he clicks on *Text Box*, then clicks on the slide in the area where he wants to put the new words. A very small box appears, which Gary can enlarge by clicking on a corner of the little box, and dragging in any direction to elongate it. He clicks and drags the box open large enough for the text he wants to place. He right clicks in the box, and then is able to enter text. He types in "Subsoil Extractors." The text automatically appears in the appropriate font of Georgia—all part of the template's complementary design.

Next, Gary changes these new words to the right size; he highlights the words, and right clicks to open a menu of ways to change the text. He increases the size to 44 point, which looks to be about the right size (it's easy to try other sizes). Gary finds it necessary to stretch the text box out a bit to allow the text to fit properly on one line. He then wants to move the text box to where the new text looks good. So he clicks to place the cursor on the outline of the text box—but not on a corner, which would change the box size—and he can click and drag the box around in the slide. Gary's on a roll. He follows the same process to add, change, and position other text elements on this title slide—including his name and the date.

On his next slide, he can set it up in one of two ways: by going to the *Home* tab and clicking on *New Slide*, or by clicking on one of the prototype slides running down the left side of the screen. When he gets the new slide on the screen, he follows the same process used on the title slide to change placeholder text, add new text boxes, type in new text, change the font size, and move the new elements into place.

About type sizes—Gary remembers from the earlier ugly slide shows how irritating it was when some of the slide text was hard to read. He also recalled from the PowerPoint class that the instructor suggested standing about 10 feet away from the computer screen periodically to look at your slides and make sure the text is visible. This test guides Gary toward making slide titles and headlines between 44–54 point, and his information bullets between 24–32 point. He also finds that his test looks at the screen help him make good judgments on whether to boldface certain elements of the text.

After completing a couple text slides, Gary decides to add a photo. In his computer's *My Pictures* folder, he has a nice shot of one of the guys in his subsoil division, wearing the digging uniform. When he comes to his third slide, he goes to the *Insert* tab, but instead of clicking *Text Box*, he clicks *Picture*. The program then prompts him through retrieval of his photo from his file, and he pastes it into the slide.

Now Gary can single click on it, and move the picture around. If he double clicks on the picture, a whole new top ribbon opens, offering *Picture Tools*. Effects can be added directly to the picture, including cropping, color adjustments, borders, and more. After reducing the size of the picture, Gary adds some text to the slide, and moves on to the next slide.

He clicks on *New Slide*, then on the *Title and Content* slide. This slide has six faint images in the center. He clicks on the faint, small bar graph-looking icon that says *Insert Chart*. He first sees a presentation datasheet, where the values are listed. By clicking in any block on this datasheet, Gary can change the values and legends on the chart. He clicks in the datasheet's various blocks, and replaces placeholder data with actual information from his subsoil extractors project. On the datasheet, he can add or delete rows or columns and change their titles to customize this generic chart to fit his needs. To delete, he selects a row or column, and right clicks for the delete menu. After making edits to the datasheet, a colorful image of a bar chart appears, with bar placeholders already graphed.

After finishing the chart slide and a couple more text slides, Gary completes his presentation. He has eight slides in all. Now Gary's ready to behold his creation. There are two ways to start the slide show: One, go to the *Slide Show* tab and click on the *From Beginning* button. The other way is faster; on the bottom ribbon, click the small icon on the far right that looks like a screen.

When the show starts, Gary is happily surprised to find that the predesigned template has built-in transitions and animations. He generally likes the movement in the slide show, which he thinks makes the presentation livelier. Then he recalls the distracting and irritating effects of excessive animation in Henry's PowerPoint disaster. So he reviews his presentation again to see if the movement seems overdone.

Gary decides the animations in his show are limited and subtle, with one exception; the initial title slide is a bit too gaudy. The transition that brings the background image onto the screen, called *Blinds*, employs a sweeping vertical effect. Gary thinks this circus-like effect is more movement than needed. After ending the slide show, with the initial slide selected back in *Normal View*, he goes to the top ribbon and changes the tab to *Transitions*. This immediately shows that the transition selected for this slide is *Blinds*.

Looking to the right on the ribbon, he sees one reason why this movement seems overdone. The *Duration* window shows that this effect lasts 1.6 seconds—a long time for a transition. Gary could reduce this time by clicking on the adjustment arrows in the duration window. But he decides to change the transition effect to something subtler. He checks out other available effects by clicking on each effect. The effects are immediately previewed on the slide each time one is selected.

After checking several of the choices, Gary picks the *Fade* effect, which operates smoothly and lasts only .7 seconds. *Fade in* is considered a default transition by many professionals, precisely because of its subtle effect. At this point, Gary breathes a sigh of relief; he's ready for his staff meeting. The entire slide show can be viewed at www.managerscommunicationtoolbox.com, as "Gary's Gamble 1." This example is not the most sophisticated PowerPoint presentation. It can get you started, however. Several enhancements can be made fairly easily, and they could make quite a difference.

## Add or Change Color

For one thing, more could be done with color in this example presentation. People have been associating colors with specific feelings since German scientist Johann Wolfgang Goethe expounded the idea in 1810. Studies and analyses in the years since have continued to explore the connotation of colors, and an American writer and industrial color consultant named Faber Birren published a definitive list of these associations in 1961 (Birren, 1961). Figure 8.3 presents a useful consensus on the feelings associated with colors.

**Figure 8.3**

Color Associations

| Color | Association | Objective Impression |
|---|---|---|
| Red | hot, blood | passionate, exciting |
| Orange | warm, autumnal | lively, energetic |
| Yellow | sunny | cheerful, inspiring |
| Green | cool, nature | refreshing, peaceful |
| Blue | tranquillity, trust | confidence, security |
| Purple | royalty, wisdom | dignified, mystic |
| White | snow | pure, clean |
| Black | night, emptiness | death, depressing |

Here's a cautionary tip for those who need to print out a PowerPoint presentation. Slides that have a dark background with contrasting light colored type look good on the screen, but do not print out well. You need to adjust before printing. Select the *View* tab on the page's top ribbon, then near the middle of the new ribbon, click on *Black and White*. You can now print out your slides without wearing out the toner cartridge in your printer. You click *Back to Color View*, or close out the application, and the slide show will return to full-color form.

## Add Video or Audio

**EXPERT TIP**

**Kimberly Zeich** is a senior Federal manager whose job involves making more than 100 presentations a year, to audiences ranging from a half dozen up to several hundred. She strongly recommends using music and video clips to give presentations an extra dimension. Most information may be presented via charts, graphs, and regular text bullets, she says, but audience comments suggest the dynamics of music or video have a very strong impact. She offers these tips to use audio or video clips in PowerPoint presentations:

- **Videos can make you look really good;** but they can make you look really bad if they don't run smoothly. When you set up at the conference or meeting, it's critical to check whether each of your clips will start and run properly.

- **Maintain your composure and a sense of humor.** If you do have a technical difficulty, the audience will remember how well you recover.

- **Remember that your actual speech is at the heart of your presentation.** The point of the audiovisual effect is to add to the confidence and conviction you project.

Inserting a video or sound clip in PowerPoint is quite simple. It can be a lot harder to make sure the clip plays properly—both in your office and when you get to the presentation site. Like doing many other things in PowerPoint, there are two ways to insert an audio or video clip. On the *Home* tab, click *New Slide*. When it opens in the main viewing pane of the program, decide if you want a title to this video, or if you want the video clip by itself. If you want a title, click in the box and replace the placeholder text with your title.

Then click on the movie reel to *Insert Media Clip*. A file selection box will open to help you find the file where you've stored the video clip. The video clip usually appears as a solid black box or as a frozen image of the initial frame of the video.

You need a usable video clip for this purpose. Obtaining video clips is a separate subject with a lot of concerns we can't cover here. There are legal issues to consider about copyright, as well as technical issues, which will determine whether you can play a video in PowerPoint. There are countless free or inexpensive clips, however, available on the Internet.

If you work a lot with videos, you'll convert video clips into usable formats. Video formats that work with PowerPoint include AVI, MPEG, and WMV.

There are many free video conversion programs on the Internet, along with plenty of advice on where to find videos. You can also record your own clips using digital cameras or a smartphone. Many of these devices can transfer video files directly to your computer, in files ready to go in PowerPoint.

Your video is now in the slide. When you move your presentation to another computer, or save it to send to someone, the video itself doesn't transfer into PowerPoint. The digital data in a video would make the file size of your PowerPoint presentation too large, causing all kinds of problems. Instead, the program inserts a signal and a digital address that tells the computer to play a video at a certain time, and where in the computer's memory to go find it.

So when you move your PowerPoint presentation off of the computer where you composed it—either copying it and emailing, or by transferring to a CD, flash media, or portable drive—you need to also transfer any supporting files, like video. It's important to transfer the supporting video file or files in a folder with the same name as the one they were in on your source computer. That helps when the PowerPoint program on the new computer goes looking for the video.

At this point, you should change the size of the video clip. This is done the same way you change the size of a photo: by clicking and dragging the little circles at the corners. Don't click on any other part of the outline of the slide; dragging from anywhere but the corners will distort the proportions of the video. You want to keep the original shape, otherwise it will look stretched and unprofessional. Again, you can move the video around just like the photo, by clicking and dragging in the center of the video box. You'll see the cursor with four black arrows come up, and then you can drag the video where you want it to go.

Now you'll see *Video Tools* above the tab *Playback*. Click the *Playback* tab and you will see a box that says *Start*. It has a dropdown menu next to it, offering: *On Click*, or *Automatically*. Now start the slide show again to see if the video plays successfully.

If all is well, your video will open and play—and you're in business. If it doesn't open, retrace your steps. Check which format the clip is: In the folder where the clip is stored, right click on the clip, and click *Properties*. If it isn't one of the PowerPoint-friendly formats listed above, the clip will need to be converted to a usable format.

## The Smart Tablet Option

For very small groups, some presenters are now using tablets. This currently has some cachet as using leading-edge technology, but it won't seem innovative for long. The following comment recently appeared on the user page for iPad's presentation software Keynote: "This app saved my butt. I forgot to make a slide show for class, but I was able to do it on the bus!" It may save you in a pinch, but your presentation would be better with proper preparation.

The tablet-size format is not great for presentations—even when your audience is just one person. We tested this by converting a couple slide shows into the correct formats, and loading them into the presentation software in our iPads. We used the Keynote app— essentially a reduced-feature version of the Apple counterpart to PowerPoint. It's quite inexpensive. It's also easy to set up and operate. But our informal test audiences found a major drawback: Seeing the image on the tablet's small format was just nowhere near as compelling as seeing an image on a typical screen or monitor. Our viewers found slides showing text to be particularly unimpressive. Slides using charts and graphs to present data were slightly more effective.

For small groups, we advise you to leave the iPad in your briefcase. Stick with the proven standards mentioned elsewhere, even if they seem old-fashioned: the blackboard to write on, the photo or book to hold up and gesture toward. These props, plus your animated verbal presentation, are the best, most natural dynamics for this audience size.

Note that the iPad can be connected to a video projector (using a proprietary iPad to VGA plug). In this configuration, it's essentially a small laptop running a low-octane version of PowerPoint with limited features. The presenter would be better served by a small laptop with the regular software. It's interesting to note that you can get an inexpensive app to turn your iPhone into a remote for the iPad, which can change slides in a Keynote presentation. While it doesn't make this approach any more useful, it *is* fun!

# WORK WITH THE NEWS MEDIA

"In the real world, the right thing never happens in the
right place and the right time. It is the job of journalists
and historians to make it appear that it has."

—*Samuel Clemens (Mark Twain)*

## In This Chapter

- Understanding the news media.
- Understanding reporter motivations.
- Reconciling your restrictions with
  reporter motivations.
- Why you should never say "no comment."
- Tips for dealing with the media.
- Tips for interviews.
- Templates to guide your responses.
- How to lessen anxiety, reduce the risk of
  being negatively portrayed, and improve
  chances of a positive outcome.

Being a source for a news story can be an exciting prospect. *All the President's Men*, an Academy Award-winning film based on the nonfiction book by journalists Carl Bernstein and Bob Woodward, captured and amplified the sense of exhilaration and trepidation people may feel when interviewed by reporters.

The story of how two enterprising reporters from *The Washington Post* unraveled the Watergate break-in and cover-up fostered legions of new journalism students, and in some ways heightened tensions surrounding communication with the media. This episode didn't invent the term "investigative reporting," but it certainly popularized the concept of journalists digging to find the truth, pressing questions in a way previously considered impolite.

A new era of "gotcha journalism" dawned in the years that followed, especially in the broadcast world where its entertainment value was recognized. Led by national programs such as *60 Minutes*, the exposé format was emulated across the nation by local television stations.

The media targeted national and municipal government officials, plus leaders of corporate giants and managers of local companies—anyone who could be caught for questionable behavior and embarrassed in front of the camera. Most of us will never have to face a *60 Minutes* crew, but many managers find it necessary—and even desirable—to speak with the media on several occasions during their careers.

Tragedy and scandal attract media attention, but there are other reasons reporters come calling. Your company could roll out a new product, or your government agency could offer a new service. Maybe there's breaking news in your field of expertise and a reporter wants opinions. Or, a television news program is developing a human interest story and wants to add you as part of their community profile. Whatever the circumstances, there are some useful techniques a manager can use.

## Define Expectations

Working with the news media brings up questions: should we expect the media to report good news and bad; can we expect reporters to get the story straight and quote accurately; can managers expect coverage when they send out announcements of new products and services? To more accurately set expectations, consider the how and why of the media—how they go about their tasks, and their motivations for doing so.

The techniques offered here have proven effective, and can be easily and immediately used by any manager. But even flawless implementation cannot guarantee positive news coverage. Unfortunately, nothing can do that.

Many large corporations employ in-house media relations experts and also contract PR agencies to maintain a positive corporate image in the news. Even this level of intensity doesn't ensure good publicity. So what can one chapter do?

A lot, by providing a focused look at media/manager communication, and then offering some templates of how to respond to typical media inquiries. This will help managers know what to expect and will give them a good starting position.

## State of the News Media Today

Especially in the broadcast world, the entertainment value of news has become increasingly important. "Once an altruistic and perhaps too idealistic profession with keen focus on balance, accuracy, and integrity, journalism is today driven by corporate profits ... news today is presented less to inform and more to titillate, seduce, and entertain," says David Henderson, a top media relations consultant. It's not that today's reporters don't have an abiding respect for truth and balance, but their first priority is getting a story that will be interesting to the public.

## There *Will* Be a Story

The media has an obligation to produce a story. A reporter typically doesn't have the option to produce a story only if the source is cooperative. A reporter is expected to get a story, period.

In normal circumstances, therefore, it's a manager's best interest to work with reporters to provide information and facilitate accuracy. In the process, the manager may be able to provide information that casts his organization in a positive light.

Another salient thing to note about the state of modern media affairs concerns speed and currency. In bygone eras, when most news was gathered and written by newspaper reporters with the luxury of larger staff and longer lead times, stories sometimes were written over a period of days. Broadcast networks were capable of reporting breaking news more rapidly. Working together, newspapers and broadcast media established a news cycle of 24 hours.

Then the advent of cable news outlets, followed by the rise of Internet news sites, accelerated the news cycle dramatically. Breaking news is now published nearly instantaneously. Traditional news outlets have reacted with efforts to continuously update stories. The next newspaper edition may not come out until the next day, and broadcast news programs may not air for several hours, but both news media outlets typically will run more timely news on companion Internet sites.

These changes are significant because managers should understand specific reporting deadlines. For cable and Internet reporters, of course, the publishing deadline will be immediately upon completion of the writing. But for a conventional broadcast or newspaper reporter, there may be a harder deadline—one that will make or break a story. Then, since there *will* be a story, a manager should make every effort to respond before the deadline.

Here are two strong and universal admonitions in working with the media. First, if you don't know the answer to a question, say so. Offer to find the answer and then provide it, but don't make one up. Second, tell the truth. Eventually, the truth will come out, and lost credibility is hard to regain.

## When It's Easy to Talk

Many interactions with the media are benign, because they involve subjects people feel comfortable talking about. But there are also controversial or difficult circumstances some managers are uneasy talking about, and on which their organizations prefer no media coverage. There are important guidelines to follow in both instances.

With easy questions, there is one trap to look out for. Naturally you'll want to cooperate, and offer the kind of energetic responses that mark sharp, self-assured managers. It must be remembered, however, that reporters—even if friendly and likable—are not there to be your friends. They do not share the goals of your organization or its managers; their objective is a story. A reporter won't alert you any time you say something they will actually use, so everything you say to them can be written about.

Besides times when you want to talk too much, there are times you don't want to talk at all. Examples of these times are: a tragedy has occurred at your work site but all the details are not available; a negative event (scandal, plant closing, and so on) is rumored and upper management wants to remain mum; a crime is being investigated, and talking about it might violate employee privacy. With challenges like this, it's understandable why the phrase "no comment" has gained such a popular following.

**EXPERT TIP**

**Joanne Richter** dealt with controversial issues for two decades as director of the Sexual Assault Treatment Center in Broward County, Florida. In addition to dealing with reporters seeking details on hundreds of individual assault cases, Richter was at ground zero for one of the most raucous media feeding frenzies in recent years: the rape trial of Patrick Kennedy Smith in Palm Beach, Florida. When the trial judge issued a gag order for officials in Palm Beach County, reporters from all over the world sought out Richter for an explanation of the legal process in rape cases, and for any other observations she could offer on sexual assault. Richter explains why you should never say "no comment":

- **You might not be able to provide specific details**. But you should be able to give them something—at least some background—that they can use to flesh out the story.

- **Reporters might find a "no comment" suspicious, or irritating**. Since a reporter doesn't find that helpful, the story might hint that you and your organization are hiding something. Even more likely, the tone of the piece will be that your organization is inept.

- **Reporters appreciate it when you try to help**. The story will often reflect that. Even if you can't answer specific questions, you can often provide general information and related facts they can use.

- **Explain the situation.** If you're prohibited from speaking about a case under court order, explain the legal situation to the reporter. If you can't reveal specifics of a case, because doing so would violate the privacy of those involved, explain this to the reporter too.

- **If possible, answer questions and provide information in generic terms** of similar cases. Preface your comments with a statement: "I can't talk about that particular case, but in similar situations I can tell you how the process usually works."

- **Offer background information** such as statistics, history, and explanations of procedures.

- **Visuals are useful to the media**. If possible, offer background photos to print reporters, and provide opportunities for television news crews to get B-roll footage.

## Rules of Engagement

From news and movies, we're familiar with reporters using unnamed sources. Someone offers to provide information to a reporter, as long as his identity as the source will not be disclosed. If this is the only way the reporter might obtain the information, she may agree to keep the source confidential.

In sophisticated political and business circles in cities like Washington and New York, there are some nuances to confidentiality agreements in providing information, expressed as "off the record," "for background," "on deep background," and "not for attribution." There are many opportunities here for misunderstanding with the reporter. Not only might the reporter have a different understanding than the manager, it also seems that reporters don't even agree among themselves.

Most people think "off the record" means that what you say won't be published at all, but reporters haven't all agreed to that definition. Amazingly, when five *Washington Post* reporters were asked what it meant to go "off the record," to go on "deep background," and three related terms, it was found that "they held widely divergent definitions" of these arrangements (Noah, 1999).

Furthermore, in a modern age of converging technologies, it's difficult to secure the confidentiality of anything typed into a computer. The best course for managers in working with the media is to remain on the record, with the knowledge that anything you say can and will be used against you in the court of public opinion. Talking to the media does put a bit of extra pressure on the normal requirement to think before you speak, but if you are careful, you can be successful.

## For All Interviews

Here are useful tips for any interview:

- The reporter is not there as your friend; don't say anything you don't want to see in print or on the air.
- Keep your answers focused and brief. Prattling along at length, in a wide-ranging manner, increases the chance you will say something you will regret.
- Don't use jargon or acronyms. The reporter may not understand, and many among the public certainly will not understand.
- Beware of reporters who are "awed by your brilliance" or "silently awaiting further disclosure." Both techniques are designed to keep you talking so you might slip up and say something you will regret.
- Bridge from inane or unfocused questions to points you'd like to make. For example: "Well the XYZ Corporation doesn't endorse products, but our testing programs provide information consumers can use to make their own judgments."
- It's fine to be friendly, but don't joke around. Something said in humor might make it into the story by accident, or because the reporter finds it just "too juicy" to leave out.

- Conclude with a simple statement summarizing or reflecting well on your mission. For example: "I'm glad we had a chance to clarify the XYZ Corporation's commitment to consumer safety."

## The Initial Contact: Templates to Guide Your Response

The initial contact from the media can be by email, telephone, or in person. Whichever one, you must immediately assess the situation to determine when and how to respond.

Return phone calls or emails promptly, but greet reporters in person immediately. You should ask the questions below to decide how quickly you need to respond to specific questions.

Questions for the Reporter:

- What's the publication, broadcast outlet, or website name, and the name of the reporter or producer?
- What's the subject of the inquiry or visit?
- Is the story for print, broadcast, or Internet? If broadcast, will the interview be live or taped?
- Is there a hard deadline for the story, such as: immediate, a few hours, or the next news cycle?
- How will the information/interview be used? (Will others be interviewed?)
- Will visuals be helpful (photos for print, background shots for broadcast)?

Answer questions to yourself after finding out the answers to the questions in the list above. Questions for You:

- Am I familiar with this publication or broadcast program?
- Is this subject a controversial or sensitive one, on which I can expect difficult questions?
- Do I actually have information on the subject, or should this inquiry be directed elsewhere?

With these basic questions answered, refer to one of the following templates: Template 1—Responding Immediately; Template 2—Short Pause Before Response; Template 3—Request for Future Interview; and Template 4—Special Considerations for Sensitive and Controversial Situations.

**Figure 9.1**

### Template 1: Respond Immediately

If the reporter is facing an imminent deadline, or if the inquiry is relatively simple and nonsensitive, it's best to respond immediately.

- Even without much time to contemplate, you should have a simple statement that summarizes or reflects well on your organization's mission.
- By asking for details about the story the reporter is working on, you can gain time to form the wording of your statements.
- Even though it may have been stated that the story is "on deadline," ask whether it will be updated at certain points—in case you can gather and provide further information, supporting data, and visuals later.
- Give the reporter a business card or spell out your name and position to help with accuracy in attribution.

**Figure 9.2**

### Template 2: Short Pause Before Response

When the inquiry or request is for real-time response rather than for a future interview, but there doesn't appear to be an immediate, hard deadline, we recommend asking the reporter for a short pause before beginning. This can easily be posed as, "I will need just three or four minutes to clear my schedule." On the telephone, offer to "call back in less than five minutes" (this can have the added benefit of verifying the reporter is authentic). If the reporter or news team is present at your work site, you might ask them to wait in a conference room or reception area "for just three or four moments while I finish something." These few minutes of prep time will help you focus.

- Compose a couple main points which you can state in a few seconds each that will summarize or reflect well on your organization's mission.
- Quickly think of any questions you may be asked and form a general idea of response.
- Have on hand a business card or sheet of paper giving the spelling of your name and position.
- Assemble any useful background brochures or similar materials about your organization and mission.
- Consider what visuals might be appropriate to offer—photographs for print media, possible video sequences for broadcast media.

**Figure 9.3**

Template 3: Request for Future Interview

A request for an interview in the future provides the luxury of time to prepare.

- Compose a couple main points which you can state in a few seconds each that will summarize or reflect well on your organization's mission. Anticipate questions you may be asked and devise succinct answers.
- Enlist help from co-workers to pose questions, while you refine making your responses concise and articulate.
- Practice stating your main points as the best way to respond to an inane or off-base question.
- Prepare a short (half-sheet of paper) list of facts giving the spelling of your name, position and—if appropriate—a brief statement of your background.
- Consider what visuals you can offer: photographs for print media, possible video sequences for broadcast media.

If the request is for an on-camera interview, prepare with the realization that your appearance will have as much impact on the audience as your words.

**Attire:**

- Dress for a conservative, professional appearance: suit or sport coat and slacks (men and women); women should avoid short skirts.
- Blue shirts show well (though they're no longer mandatory, thanks to better cameras); avoid stripes and plaids.
- If you normally wear a uniform, or clinical or technical attire (lab coat, surgical garb), wear a fresh set.
- Limit jewelry; avoid large items and highly reflective pieces.
- Steer clear of any clothing or accessory that will detract from the appearance of competence and sincerity.

**Makeup:**

- If in studio, the station staff may offer simple facial makeup. Men should accept, since makeup will help you look good in bright studio lights.
- For women, normal makeup is usually sufficient, using matte finish to avoid shine.

**Verbal Responses and Body Language:**

- Take a deep breath and try to relax just before the interview begins.
- Unless the subject is somber or controversial, smile when you're first addressed on camera.
- Keep your responses and statements extremely short and to the point (sound bites for television run less than 10 seconds).
- When speaking, be animated; use gestures and facial expressions to put life in your words.
- Focus your eyes on the interviewer (looking up or off to the side makes you look shifty-eyed).

**Figure 9.4**

Template 4: Special Considerations for Sensitive and Controversial Situations

The media's appetite for controversy is a strong motivation for reporters to press questions hard, sometimes past the point of courtesy. Here are some techniques for such circumstances:

- Correct an allegation or misconception built into the question at the beginning of your answer. For example: "Your premise is incorrect that there have been past inaccuracies in XYZ's research, as proven by our accreditation by the National Academy of Sciences, but let's clarify your specific question with some recent data…"
- Don't lose your temper. Maintaining a calm, professional demeanor serves to dampen over-assertive behavior by reporters and projects sincerity.
- When asked negative and contentious questions, recast the question in a way that sets up a more positive or neutral answer. For example, if asked, "Aren't some manufacturers hiding behind your company's lax consumer reviews to produce unsafe products?" Then restate, "You're asking if independent scientific evaluation of products has an influence on manufacturers, and our data indicate that…"
- Don't accept an artificial either/or position constructed by the reporter. For example, "This is not an issue of only doing honest research *or* recommending products. We believe our valid research is a recommendation to help consumers choose."
- Don't answer a hypothetical question. If asked, "How would you feel if a large number of people made purchases based on your company's recommendation, and later were harmed by those products?" You might answer, "You've asked a hypothetical question, presenting a scenario that never occurred… we can better spend our time talking about real events, and real data we use to evaluate products."
- Continue bridging from contentious questions to answers citing your main points, summarizing and casting positive light on your organization's mission. Don't be afraid to repeat yourself; stating your points repeatedly in different ways increases chances your points will sink in with print reporters, or survive editing for broadcast.

# THINK LIKE A MANAGER

"The greatest difficulty in the world is not for people to accept new ideas, but to make them forget their old ideas."

—*John Maynard Keynes*

---

**In This Chapter**

- Why sound thinking is important.
- The four basic thinking tools: strategize, analyze information, be creative, and arrive at a decision.

---

Jeff Immelt has been the CEO of the General Electric Company since 2002. When Immelt took over, he believed GE was becoming a boring place to work, and that GE's managers were afraid to take risks. Soon after taking charge, Immelt took a radical step. "We had to have some way to pull ideas out of the pile," he said, "make sure they were funded, and really try to redefine what it means to innovate in a big company (Byrne, 2005)." So he created a structure that not only encouraged his managers to spend part of the time thinking about new ideas—it forced them to do so.

Immelt created Commercial Council, which included leaders of different segments of GE's business. The Council was designed to increase the company's historic growth rate of about 4 percent per year. Council members "learn from each other, challenge each other, and root for each other (GE, 2007)." Perhaps more importantly, council members are required to regularly submit "imagination breakthrough" proposals to take GE into new lines of business, geographic areas, or customer bases. Immelt is forcing his senior leaders to think hard about the future, and to take risks to help the company grow. He is also putting his money where his mouth is by funding many of the projects.

Immelt's requirement that his senior managers think deeply about GE's business and how it can grow is surprisingly unusual in the business world. Although no company will ever say it outright, original thinking is often discouraged in favor of pressures to meet the bottom line, or to get a new product to market, or to discount the long run in favor of immediate rewards.

Thinking is hard. If you want a successful career, however, the ability to think clearly and strategically is a must. Sound thinking skills are important in every manager's day-to-day activities: managing time, making choices among alternatives, delegating responsibility or authority, and negotiating with others. Managers are also required to think about strategic responsibilities: developing office goals, participating in planning sessions, analyzing the success and failure of programs and people, and brainstorming new ideas.

Managers who think clearly and well will shine in these situations. Whether or not their company actively pursues a strategy like GE's, they will have a better time than those who "go along to get along."

## How to Strategize

What is strategy and how can a new manager become good at it? Strategizing is the ability to plan for the future; to build—as football teams do—a game plan that will enable you to win. You may want to increase your company's market share, or your staff's job satisfaction, or your organization's reputation in its community, or simply develop a plan that will enable you to complete a project on time and within budget.

Managers who are good strategic thinkers have all of the communication skills. They *read* widely on anything remotely connected to their work. They *talk* to people regularly, and seek out their opinions. When they *speak*, they ask questions, and challenge assumptions. And they *listen* carefully to their customers, at seminars, and whenever they get the opportunity to learn from experts in their field. In short, strategic thinkers are always looking for more information they can use when the opportunity presents itself.

There are, of course, many ways strategic thinkers create strategies, but here's a four-step process to use.

- Analyze your current situation.
- Develop options for change.
- Evaluate the options you've selected.
- Pick the best option or options.

A significant tool organizations use to analyze their current situation is a SWOT (Strengths, Weaknesses, Opportunities, and Threats) analysis. A consultant named Albert S. Humphrey developed the tool, which originated at Stanford University in the 1960s. SWOT analyses are used both in business and in government for projects large and small, but the first step in any analysis is always the same: Clearly identify the planning objective.

Knowing where you're going is critical to the remainder of the SWOT process, which involves identifying

- the *strengths* of your organization that provide it with advantages other organizations don't have
- the *weaknesses* that give other firms advantages your organization lacks

- the *opportunities* that exist outside the organization to accomplish the task
- the *threats* from outside the organization that will make it more difficult for success.

In identifying *strengths*, look at tasks your group or organization does better than anything else, and think about resources available to you that others don't have or have to pay more to get. Also, try to discern why people buy the products you already sell or use the services you already provide, as opposed to those of your competitors.

In looking at *weaknesses*, think of areas you've previously considered that need improvement; people on your staff or elsewhere who will not be able to rise to the occasion; and strengths your competitors have that you lack—especially those that enable them to make a profit at your expense.

*Opportunities* include new advantages brought by technology, government policy, or demographic shifts. Here's where staying up-to-date on what's happening in your company and your business pays off—as does watching the competition, continually assessing your customers' attitudes, and reading widely in your area and on business in general.

Finally, *threats* include obsolete technology; your competitors' work; and limits on available funding to accomplish your task.

In accomplishing a SWOT analysis, use facts, not opinions, for example: "Last year, we sold $250 million worth of widgets to Uganda, nearly 95 percent of their total imports of widgets," instead of "We do a whole lot of business in Africa, which our competitors don't." If you do the analysis as a group, and everyone provides input, don't accept the long lists of ideas. Instead, keep cutting until only the most significant factors remain. And don't try to get everyone in the company involved, unless you have to. It's a lot easier to do a SWOT analysis for one product than for an entire organization's work.

There are, of course, many other planning tools companies use to analyze their current situation and assess opportunities for change. The "Porter's Five Forces" model, for example, was developed by Michael E. Porter of Harvard Business School in 1979. It helps determine whether a company should move into a new market, or improve their position in current markets. The Delta Model is a way to develop strategies by looking at issues from a customer-centered viewpoint. And the National Diamond, also developed by Michael Porter, helps to analyze a firm's ability to function in a national marketplace and an international market. But the SWOT analysis is a simple, flexible, and useful analytic tool. Try it—it works!

## Develop Options

Once you assess the current situation, you should develop options that help meet your goal. Option development is nearly always done better in a group than individually. Groups allow people with different backgrounds to bring their knowledge, experience, and skills to a project. This generates alternative points of view or solutions to the problem.

When your group is assembled, many techniques can get everyone's creative juices flowing. Brainstorming—in which group members are asked for solutions to a problem, and are then given a short amount of time to call out a response—is frequently used.

**Figure 10.1**

Analyzing Information

Way back at the beginning of the computer age in the 1970s, programmers developed the acronym GIGO, meaning "garbage in, garbage out." While it originally referred to the fact that computers will find a way to process any kind of input data, we've come to learn that if the input data are no good, the answers that come out will be no better. Within a few short years, this phrase referred to all kinds of human behavior, and especially what happens when people make decisions using wrong, incomplete, or imprecise data—the decisions come out equally incorrectly.

Herbert E. Meyer, a former special assistant to the director of the Central Intelligence Agency and associate editor of *Fortune* magazine, has written a short pamphlet entitled *"How to Analyze Information: A Step-by-Step Guide to Life's Most Vital Skill* (Meyer, 2010)." Meyer's pamphlet begins with the assertion that never before has so much information been available, so easily and inexpensively, about so many subjects. Using information properly, however, requires the ability to analyze it properly.

It's vitally important, especially in the Internet era, to consider the source of the information. The web has made everyone a publisher, and a place where people can write anything they want. Data from government agencies can usually be relied upon, as can data from colleges and universities. Use multiple sources; don't rely on just one.

Make sure you know what questions you're asking before beginning your analysis. When you're collecting data, separate what's essential from what's nice to know, and separate facts from opinions. Remember that facts can be—and often are—selectively used by authors to support their theses. Check sources, and be attentive to any biases an author may exhibit.

Once you've collected the data, organize it in a way that is usable to you. Look for patterns in data that will help you make sense of what you've gathered. Take note of things that are similar or different, or are related in some way. Look for causes and effects, relationships, patterns, and trends.

Finally, interpret your results. Come to a conclusion that will guide your future actions. Meyer suggests that the final ingredient in analyzing information is your own judgment. If the data tell you one thing, and your instincts tell you another, don't disregard what your inner voice is telling you when making a final decision or recommendation.

If you facilitate a brainstorming session, encourage everyone to actively call out ideas. They should say whatever comes to mind. The wilder the better! Don't ask for explanation, just write down everything—and don't allow any criticism at this time. Ask someone outside the group to record, and use a flipchart to write down everyone's thoughts. There should be no editing or worrying about duplicate ideas at this time.

You could also do a round-robin session; ask people one at a time for their ideas, and continue until everyone says "pass." This way the session is not dominated by only a few participants. Unfortunately, then you put pressure on people to say something—anything—when it's their turn to speak. It also makes it harder for people to build off others' ideas, as they do in traditional brainstorming sessions.

One of the 20th century's greatest inventions, the sticky note, is another way to brainstorm. Give everyone a pad to have them write their ideas down, and then post them on a chart. Try to give everyone a different color—if not, have them initial their submissions on the back of the note.

Once you've developed options from brainstorming, they need to be clarified. To do this, first assign numbers to each of the options you've developed. Give people a chance to think about them, and then—one at a time—ask them to identify any option they'd like clarified. Only the person who originated the option should respond—and that response is not open to debate. Continue to go around the group until everyone passes and no one still has questions. If time is a problem, place a limit on the number of rounds before you start the process, not afterward.

Then the group should look at the options and search for similarities or duplicates. Everyone—again, one at a time—can suggest items to be either combined or removed from the list. If the people who suggested the items agree, then they can be combined. Too much discussion about whether an item really can be combined with another means it probably can't.

Brainstorming should provide you with viable options to attack the problem. The Management Standards Consultancy (2007) suggests a three-step method to begin the process of determining which of the options you've brainstormed will actually work.

- Is the option *acceptable*; does it help solve the problem?
- Is the option *feasible*; can it actually be done?
- Is the option *safe*? If things go wrong, can you tolerate the consequences?

To determine whether an option is *acceptable*, the Consultancy suggests you ask the following questions.

- Does it meet your technical requirements?
- Does it improve the quality of products or services?
- Does it improve your ability to serve customers, your profitability, and your dependability?
- Does it increase your flexibility—and does it do this at an acceptable cost?

To check *feasibility*, look at whether you have the skills—human and technical—the capacity, and the financial resources to implement the option. Can you tolerate the amount of change that it calls for, and does it fit with your organization's priorities and values?

And finally, to see if the option is *safe*, examine how the decision might go wrong, the impact that would have, and whether your company can tolerate the worst-case scenario.

Reject any option that does not meet all three criteria. If none of the options survive, it's time to get more information, develop new options, or reconsider the problem you're trying to solve.

Once you're down to only a few options. you must decide, unless you are only required to make a recommendation. We'll discuss decision-making skills in more detail, but for now you should evaluate your final set of options in three ways:

- Are you confident this option will achieve what it is supposed to achieve?
- Is now the time to do this?
- Will your staff and supervisors understand why you're doing this, and what will they think?

If everything checks out, in your own mind and in the minds of everyone with whom you're sharing decision-making responsibility, then go for it.

## EXPERT TIP

**Anthony J. Principi** is a former member of the President's Cabinet, the former executive chairman of QTC Management, and the former vice president for government affairs for Pfizer. "I do my thinking in the very early morning," he says. "Once I read my first email, or start my first meeting, my time is no longer my own." Other aids to his thought process include:

- **Placing trust in those with whom he works**. "Leadership is defined by the people with whom you surround yourself. I choose to hire smart people— people who knew they weren't going to be thrown out of my office if they came up with an idea that challenged the status quo."

- **Looking to smart people for guidance**. Listen to everyone's viewpoint before making a decision. "In the end, I always held myself accountable for the decisions I made."

- **Believing that the decision you're making is the right one**. "Making a decision is a relatively simple process. Get the right people, challenge them, figure out the right thing to do, and then make a decision accordingly. And if your decision turns out to be wrong, own up to it and change course."

- **Having fun**. "Do things together, and share the credit. Show people that you like them, make sure they know you appreciate them, and great ideas will flow."

## Business Tools to Collect Information

While more information than ever is available on the Internet and elsewhere, businesses frequently find they require specialized information that hasn't been developed by anyone else. Here are some tools to get the additional information you need.

**Questionnaires and surveys.** These allow you to gain information on what people think about your issue, how they feel about it, and what they know about it. Surveys can be conducted in person, on the telephone, and via mail or email. There are websites, such as *www.surveymonkey.com*, that will help you create and conduct Internet-based surveys with ease.

Surveys can be done quickly, even with many responders. If they are constructed correctly, it's easy to analyze the results. They're great for determining your needs; gathering baseline data so you can measure your progress against your goals; finding out what other people think about your organization; and getting information from large groups. They can, however, be costly, and most don't allow respondents to give you detailed responses.

**Focus groups.** These are people who are brought together to answer questions about their perceptions, opinions, beliefs, and attitudes. Sessions are conducted by trained moderators and usually consist of six to 10 people. They are particularly useful in getting feedback from users of your products and services. You can assess the need for a new product, gather opinions on an existing one, or gain qualitative information about how your unit, product, or company is perceived.

In a group setting, participants tend to be more open and honest than in one-on-one interviews. The interaction among participants may take the discussion in unexpected directions, which may be rewarding and get you unexpected information. Group discussions, however, are time-consuming to put together, and need to be conducted by facilitators trained to work with groups.

**Interviews.** By talking to people one at a time, you can get the information you need from the people you need to get it from. In-person interviews allow you to hear the person you're speaking with and allow her to go into detail. They also allow the interviewer to observe the nonverbal responses of the interview subject: expressing her opinion passionately; using gestures; smiling or frowning; pacing around while thinking or talking. The way things are said often is more significant than the words.

Interviews, however, are time-consuming—and sometimes costly. Interviewers must be trained not to let their biases show in order to avoid prejudicing the respondents' answers, so don't conduct interviews yourself without proper training.

**Community meetings.** Many government agencies and some other businesses conduct discussion sessions to check on the communities they serve. Community meetings (or town halls) are also a great way to talk to large groups at one time. Sometimes these are virtual—using technology to allow people all over the world to participate.

Whether a community meeting is held for an external or internal audience, the objectives are usually the same. These meetings are especially good for promoting new initiatives or setting goals, and for encouraging the community to help develop an initiative or celebrate its accomplishment. Community meetings can also be part of the decision-making process if attendees provide ideas about a problem the organization faces.

This type of meeting allows opinions and ideas to be collected from a wide range of people. It also gets them involved in the process early on, and creates interest in any initiatives. Downsides of community meetings include the limited time they allow to discuss issues of importance, and that some people with useful viewpoints may be afraid to provide those in front of large groups.

All of these techniques have their pros and cons, but each should be part of your information-gathering toolbox. Usual information gathering includes literature and Internet searches. Also, in using government documents and reviewing other data your company may have available, you should be able to get the information to conduct a sound analysis of the problem you need to solve.

## Creativity

It isn't easy being creative. Managers are constantly exhorted to come up with great new ideas on command. Despite the difficulties in creative thinking, there are ways to get your creative juices flowing, and to maximize the chances you'll hit upon an idea that is not only new, but will actually work.

The first way to come up with creative ideas is to brainstorm in a group setting. Remember the rule about encouraging wild ideas—this cannot be overemphasized. Sometimes, the craziest ideas are the most creative—not what you'll get from ideas that only involve incremental change. It's also important in brainstorming sessions to do all you can to eliminate individual status from the room. People tend to defer to the senior person. Once the boss has spoken, they take it as the right direction in which to look or think. That can significantly inhibit creativity.

Along those lines, it's a great idea to ask as many people as you can what they think. Talk to your customers, to the people who work directly with customers, to everyone you can get ahold of. You'll find everyone has a different perspective, and those perspectives will help you think differently. Some people will have great ideas to help you accomplish your goals. A nurse at a large hospital, for example, was concerned that some patients were receiving medications intended for someone else, so she came up with a system of bar coding the identification tag on every patient's wrist and comparing it with bar codes on the medications. Now a widely accepted practice, her idea saved many lives.

If you're thinking on your own, though, and looking for inspiration, start out by doing something a little different. Take a different route to work; park farther out in the parking lot; take a walk at 10 a.m. to clear your head; relocate your desk in your office; hang up a new photograph; change your work hours slightly. Just making a few changes to your daily routine can change your entire outlook.

Don't think too hard about being creative. All of us have probably experienced the paradox that the harder we try to think creatively, the fewer ideas come out. Keep a pad handy at all times, even by your bedside. If an idea comes to you, or even a fragment of an idea, jot it down immediately. And don't spend all your time obsessing about problems you're facing, even if there's a time crunch. Your brain needs time to relax and renew itself. Return to the problem only when you feel refreshed. Stay away from your smartphone at night. Don't watch too much news during your downtime (or too much TV of any kind—listening to music instead relaxes you and stimulates creativity). Don't be a person who never takes a vacation from work. That attitude takes its toll in the long run.

If a solution to a problem doesn't come to you immediately, put it aside for a while. Give yourself a fixed amount of time to think about the issue, and then stop. If the answer doesn't come now, it'll come later—perhaps in a blinding flash of inspiration. Train yourself to think creatively by taking a problem that already has a solution, and looking at alternate ways that problem could have been solved. Then refine your alternate solutions to make them faster, cheaper, and better than the solution you've already got. Do this exercise a few minutes a day and the patterns of thinking you've established will help you when you've got a significant problem to solve.

Finally, just as you encourage a brainstorming group to create wild ideas, don't censor your own crazy thoughts. Instead of dwelling on the reasons things won't work, get enthusiastic about the possibilities. And banish negative and restrictive phrases like "It's never been done before," from your internal dialogue and from your discussions with others.

## Make a Decision

It would be a wonderful thing if—after identifying your options, sorting out the information you've got, and thinking creatively—the solution to your problem was so evident anyone could see it. Sometimes, it even works out that way. Often, however, you'll need to make a decision between two or more solutions, each of which appear to be correct. How do you make the right call? Management schools teach elaborate decision-making methods, such as Bayesian logic and decision trees. There are, however, some less elaborate methods of reaching decisions in a more down-to-earth manner. Making the right decisions in a simple, practical manner on a day-to-day basis is what being a manager is all about.

First off, before you make an important decision, clear your head. If you feel the weight of the world on your shoulders, take a walk. Go to the gym. Check out a humor website, or do whatever it is that relaxes you. Being in a good mood definitely helps you make good decisions.

The second step in making a difficult decision is one most people are familiar with: List all of your alternatives. What different decisions can you make in your situation? Decisions in business rarely involve simple "yes" or "no" answers—and it's impossible to keep every alternative in your head. Once you've written down all your choices, think through each one, and make some notes. List the pros and cons of each alternative, and quickly eliminate those that have more cons than pros.

Don't be selective while making your list. Don't be biased in favor of certain solutions, or disregard arguments that support conclusions you don't think will work. Don't end your search when you've found an answer that just might work—instead, keep going until you've thoroughly explored every alternative.

Be wary of peer pressure—this is your decision, so don't make it because you know someone else will approve. Even if you've done group brainstorming, only one person is accountable in most decisions. If you're that person, you're the one who has to decide. Of course, that doesn't mean including others in the process was a waste. It'll be much easier to get people's buy-in to your decision if they've been included in the process.

The third step is to stop collecting information about your decision. The phrase "analysis paralysis" is about delaying decisions indefinitely—just waiting for one more piece of information, or one more person's input. Sooner or later the time comes to move forward; in most cases, the wrong decision is better than no decision at all. Every difficult decision is made with some degree of uncertainty. If there was no uncertainty, the decision would be simple.

The fourth and final step is to consult your gut. All your formal analysis, all your information, all your list making should make you comfortable with the decision you've chosen. If your intuition tells you you're doing the wrong thing, however, you'd better listen. Sometimes your subconscious has worked through an issue in ways your conscious mind cannot describe. Clear your mind of everything but your decision; visualize outcomes in detail; think about what a role model of yours would have done.

Then, make a choice. Even if you're still not sure what you want to do, go forward. Don't let fear stop you. Separate yourself from the emotions of the moment, and, as the Nike brand says: "Just do it." If you really can't decide between two alternatives, ask a few people you trust what they would do if they were in your shoes. If it's any consolation to you, if you've spent a long time on a decision and it's still close, the chances are both alternatives are equally good.

Once you've made the decision, forget about the alternatives you were considering. Don't second-guess yourself. Don't worry about new information that comes in later on, just do all you can to make sure your decision is implemented in the way you foresaw it. Follow up by evaluating both the decision you made and the process by which you made it to see what you learned and how you can do better. And if you find you're not getting anywhere near the results you expected, don't hesitate to start the process again and try something else.

## CHAPTER 11

# GET OTHERS TO THINK

"If I have seen further than others, it is by standing upon the shoulders of giants."

—*Sir Isaac Newton*

---

### In This Chapter

- Why it's important to get others to think.
- Get staff involved in all of your work.
- How to run staff meetings properly.
- How to create a positive and involved environment.
- Allow people to act independently and share the responsibilities of decision making.

---

Michael Jordan may be the greatest basketball player who ever lived. His deadly shooting eye, his strength, and his will to win created a player who simply could not be stopped from scoring points when he set his mind to it. His gifts were evident even when he was a teenager in high school.

Before his professional career with the Chicago Bulls, Jordan attended the University of North Carolina. When he was a freshman, he was told to take a seat on the bench during practice. He sat and watched his teammates play, and finally he asked his coach, the legendary Dean Smith, why he had had to sit. "Michael," Smith said, "if you can't pass, you can't play!"

Even the Michael Jordans of this world cannot achieve much without help. The famed inventor and genius Thomas Alva Edison, when asked why he had 21 assistants, responded, "If I could solve all the problems myself, I would."

It is important to improve your own ability to think, but it's also important to get other people—especially your team members—to think. New managers may believe that it's their job to see the big picture and develop the road their staff will follow, but that's a sure path to failure. Do you really want a staff that's always dependent on you for direction, and for answers? If that's the kind of support you've got, you'll never have time to do anything else but tell them what to do.

## EXPERT TIP

As the head of civil litigation practice and a partner in the law firm of Bracewell and Giuliani, **Larry Silverman** has represented many high-profile cases in significant disputes. In a profession that places a premium on clear, innovative thought, Silverman has helped many young lawyers to think for themselves. Here's how:

- **He teaches by example**. "When I'm training new associates, I ask them to take part in a case I'm working on. The first couple of decisions that come up, I make myself—and I explain what we're going to do and why. Around the third or fourth time a decision comes up, I ask them to figure out what they should do by themselves. The good ones will try to figure out what to do based on what I did."

- **He turns problem-bringers into problem-solvers**. "I know all our clients have problems—or they would have done the work themselves. Our firm is paid to find innovative solutions to problems—we're not being paid to do the obvious."

- **He believes experience is the best teacher**. "Pro bono work (performed voluntarily and free of charge) gives young lawyers the opportunity to make decisions themselves without the pressure of having to deal with a paying client. I still supervise them closely, though."

## Get Your Staff Involved

**Signs of unmotivated employees:** "That's not in my job description." "We've never done things that way before." "I've got five years, six months, and 23 days to retirement, and I can't wait." Those people will only do what they need to in order to get by—and sometimes not even that much. It's tough to get people with those attitudes to think independently, or to help you shape the direction of your organization in a positive way.

Few of these people were born with built-in negativity. Most came into your organization with a positive attitude: eager to be part of the team, make new friends, and contribute to the success of the group. Something happened along the way to make them lose their motivation.

It's your job as a manager to nurture or restore their motivation or to get rid of those who resist. It's just as important, however, to maintain the positive attitude of your new hires, and to encourage those long-term employees who are still motivated to do even more in support of your company's goals.

# Run Staff Meetings Properly

Let's face it—most people hate staff meetings. They consider them boring, a waste of time, a drain on creativity, and a good place to practice their doodling skills. Larry Silverman calls as few meetings as possible, because "our clients don't want to pay for them."

Meetings can be valuable, however, if conducted properly. Staff meetings can be a great way for you to constantly communicate with your staff, and a way for them to communicate with each other. Handled properly, they can encourage original thinking; develop and keep open lines of communication with your staff; and increase the amount of recognition you offer to staff members who have done good work.

Most importantly, staff meetings should energize attendees and renew their sense of commitment to the organization's goals. Quite frankly, most staff meetings don't do that. You know you've got a problem when people regularly show up late, or find an excuse not to show up at all.

Make sure every staff meeting has a plan, a purpose, and an agenda. Agendas are important, so people can prepare themselves by knowing what's going to be discussed ahead of time. If there are materials to be distributed, send them out in advance. If you find out your staff hasn't read the material, let them know you aren't pleased—and dissolve the meeting until a future date. Meetings are for discussion, not one-way communication, or they shouldn't be taking place at all.

If you're asking people to make presentations as part of the agenda, tell them how long they have to speak, and hold them to it. Don't let people pontificate or go on tangents. One manager we know brings a long hook to meetings, and if a presenter goes on too long, she ostentatiously displays it. She's never actually given anyone the hook—but no one doubts that she can, or will. If time is running out on a useful subject, set another time for the discussion to continue, or set up a small group to look into the issue further.

Try to link your agenda with your organization's mission. If you're trying to increase sales, for example, always have some aspect of selling on your agenda. Outside guests both from your industry and other parts of your organization can add value; the presence of visitors often encourages people to feel pride in their organization.

Staff meetings should be held regularly; if you've got a small staff, weekly meetings are probably best. Whatever schedule you've set, don't continually cancel or postpone them—your team will see that as a lack of respect for them and for their time. Start and end meetings on time. Round tables are good for meetings, because they encourage everyone to participate; auditoriums or a bunch of chairs facing a podium give people the sense they're being lectured to. Better still is a U-shaped table or horseshoe arrangement: people are encouraged to participate, but the person at the head of the "U" is clearly in charge.

If you've got a choice, try to schedule meetings on Friday afternoons—assuming you can get the key people you need together, not an easy task in this time of compressed work schedules and working from home. The advantage is that there are likely fewer phone calls or other interruptions. This schedule also allows you to review what's been accomplished, and to set plans for the week ahead.

Make sure people come on time, and don't recap for people who show up late, because it disrespects those who made the effort to be on time. Bringing food is always a good idea. It puts participants in a better mood. You can put a cookie jar in the middle of the table and fine people who come late—perhaps a dollar a minute. Use the money in the cookie jar to pay for the refreshments.

For virtual staff meetings, make sure everyone has read-ahead material as early as possible. Be careful to monitor the group discussion. People in the physical room sometimes crowd out participants who follow the discussion by phone or videoconference. Make sure people don't talk over one another.

As a leader, your job is to control the discussion: ask good questions, get feedback from everyone, and keep discussions from getting off track. Be alert to anyone who tries to dominate the meeting. Offer to meet with that person individually to discuss her points after the meeting is over. You may have to soothe the employee you've shut down afterward, but everyone else will appreciate it.

Finally, follow up after meetings. If you and your staff have agreed on a course of action, make sure the person tasked with that responsibility is doing what he agreed to do. Don't let things vanish into thin air—asking someone to take minutes ensures having a follow-up checklist. At your next meeting, report back on progress, so everyone knows you hold people accountable.

Remember that a lack of structure will yield a lack of results. Good meetings, on the other hand, will stimulate your staff to think as a team, not as individuals; they will give everyone the big picture; and they will keep the lines of communication and creativity wide open.

## Create an Involved Environment

Thomas J. Watson was the founder and first president of IBM. Watson used the slogan "THINK" to motivate and inspire IBM's staff. He made sure the company's stationery, pads, and every room in every IBM building carried that word. Even today, more than 50 years after Watson's death, THINK is an important part of IBM's culture.

Watson was once asked if he was going to fire an employee who made a mistake that cost the company $600,000. "No," he replied. "I just spent $600,000 training him. Why would I want somebody else to hire his experience?" He also said "All the problems of the world could be settled easily if people were only willing to think. The trouble is that people very often resort to all sorts of devices in order not to think, because thinking is such hard work."

By encouraging your employees to make decisions themselves and asking them to share in the hard work of thinking, you run many risks. You lose some control over the process. Someone else decides the outcome of a problem, not you. You usually add time to the process, since it's likely your staff will take more time to decide things than you will. As Watson learned to his chagrin, sometimes people make the wrong decision, and that reflects badly on you. And finally, your staff may make a decision that isn't terrible, but isn't the best decision either, and you're the one who has to live with it.

According to Peter Barron Stark, a management consultant and co-author of the book *The Competent Leader*, there are many reasons why the benefits of empowering employees through decision making outweigh the risk (Stark, 2011). You make employees feel valued and trusted; you help them learn and grow; and you encourage them to take action on their own. After all, if someone else makes the decisions, why should your staff think independently?

When talking to your staff, ask questions and listen hard to the answers. Don't interrupt people before they finish speaking: Make sure they complete their thoughts before you respond. Understand that what people say to you is important to them, even if it doesn't seem important to you.

Above all, create an involved environment by trusting your co-workers and subordinates. The writer Ernest Hemingway said: "The best way to find out if you can trust somebody is to trust them." Trust in their abilities, trust in their willingness to do what they've said they will do, trust that they will share information with you and that given a chance, they will do the right thing—and they more than likely will.

Michael Jordan learned to trust his teammates, and as a result, led by Coach Dean Smith, they won an NCAA basketball championship. Jordan and his teammates later won six championship rings in the National Basketball Association. Value your staff, hold productive meetings, and trust them to make the right decisions unless and until they prove they can't—and you, too, can be a champion.

---

**Figure 11.1**

### Seven Ways to Value Your Staff

There are lots of ways managers can communicate to team members how important and valued they are, and how their contributions are appreciated. Here are a few.

**Say thank you—often.** Achievements take place every day. They should be lauded and celebrated: in person, in staff meetings, and wherever the opportunity presents itself. Too many managers, especially new ones, don't get thanked for their own hard work by their bosses. Because of this, they resist thanking members of their staff. It's the wrong attitude and the wrong answer. Whenever you can, put your praise in writing, and don't forget to send a copy to the employee's file.

**Pay attention to people's workspace.** Employees are sensitive to their work environment. Tiny cubicles, uncomfortable chairs, and restrictive rules about plants and personal photos are all significant demotivators. You may not have responsibility for establishing those rules, or deciding how large a cubicle your employees have, but your input will be important to your own supervisors. Managers tend to think of environmental issues as less significant than many others, but employees don't. Do what you can to make people feel at home.

---

**Figure 11.1 continued**

**Give employees the chance to be leaders.** There's no better way to get employees to think than by giving them the opportunity to lead others. Form teams to solve specific problems, and give different staff members the opportunity to be in charge. Empower them to make decisions. Give them permission to challenge you when they think you are wrong.

**Listen to what your staff has to say.** Pay full attention to what your staff tells you. Take notes, so they know you take their concerns seriously. If they want to talk when you can't provide full attention, give them a specific time to return.

**Be enthusiastic.** Enthusiasm is contagious. If you show passion for your work, appreciation for what others do, and gratitude for what's been done for you, you can motivate others to do more. The theologian Dr. Norman Vincent Peale said," Enthusiasm spells the difference between mediocrity and accomplishment." Be careful, though—not everyone, including some of your best-performing staff, may share your approach. But enthusiasm sparks creativity, and if your goal is to get your staff to participate in strategic thinking, having an emotional investment in your work is key.

**Help others to be successful.** If you want your staff to help you succeed, you've got to help them succeed as well. Always try to help your co-workers improve their skills, and quickly point out things that need improvement. Help people get what *they* value from work, such as recognition for a job well done, increased responsibility, and the opportunity to learn. That puts them on the path to helping you get what's important to you, which is usually results. Don't give up, and don't let others give up either. According to the famed motivational speaker Zig Ziglar, "You will get everything in life that you want if you just help enough other people get what they want."

**Be positive.** Say positive things about your staff, especially in the presence of senior managers. If you don't have something good to say about someone, don't say anything. Don't blame everyone else for your problems; take responsibility for your own shortcomings. Tell people what can be done—not what can't be done. Suggest alternatives if what people suggest just won't work, and be helpful and encouraging whenever you can.

Taken together, this set of behaviors sends an important message to your staff. It shows respect for people with whom you work, and demonstrates that their contributions are appreciated. It is the best way to keep that motivation from the first day on the job in individuals, and to rekindle that flame in those who have lost it. Motivated staff will do what needs to be done, and will always be part of the solution, not part of the problem.

# MANAGE YOUR BOSS

"The man who knows how will always have a job. The man who also knows why will always be his boss."

—*Ralph Waldo Emerson*

---

### In This Chapter

- Why you still have to manage your boss.
- How to manage your boss.
- How and when to bring problems to your boss.
- How to address issues constructively.
- How to address concerns about your boss with others in the company.

---

It would be wonderful if people formed favorable impressions of others solely on their accomplishments. But there's more to it than that. First impressions are important. As the magazine *Psychology Today* points out, "humans have developed the ability to quickly decide whether a new person will hurt us or enrich us—judgments that had lifesaving ramifications in an earlier era (Flora, 2004)." More important, however, is the relationship you develop with your boss over time. It's the most important relationship you have in your job.

As a successful employee, you learned—possibly through painful experience—what it took to work successfully with your bosses: what made them happy; what they expected of you; and how to provide the kind of support that helped you *and* your boss succeed. But now you're a boss yourself, and that is over and done with, right?

Of course that's not true. Even the president of the United States answers to the American people. CEOs of Fortune 500 companies answer to investors and to boards of directors. Even self-employed people have bosses. As Sam Walton, the founder of Wal-Mart, once said: "There is only one boss—the customer. And he can fire everybody in the company from the chairman on down, simply by spending his money somewhere else."

So you still have a boss with whom you need to manage your relationship, even as a supervisor yourself. And if you are not managing your entire company, you are likely dealing with a second-level supervisor: someone whose job it is to supervise managers like you. These are almost always experienced people, important agents of management, ideally with a great deal of knowledge and expertise. They train you in your work, make sure your team's performance is meeting the company's expectations—and are the people to whom your staff members almost always go first when they want to complain about you!

As a manager, you start to get invited to higher-level meetings. Senior managers who attend such meetings will be those making decisions about your future career, and whether you yourself will become a second-level supervisor, or higher. Your contact with them probably was quite limited before you were given supervisory responsibilities, with little opportunity to work directly with them. Now, their good opinion of you may be as important, if not more important, than that of your immediate supervisor.

### EXPERT TIP

"People don't quit their jobs, they quit their bosses," says **Arthur S. Hamerschlag**, a principal with the MITRE Corporation. In his 40-year career with the federal government and private industry, including three years as chief of staff for the nation's largest healthcare organization, Hamerschlag has had more than his share of good and bad supervisors. Here are his tips for establishing and maintaining good relationships with all kinds of bosses.

- **Pay attention**. Understand where the boss is going—and why. "It took me a long time to listen—really listen—to the boss, especially when he and I were not on the same page."

- **Build a relationship based on trust**. Make sure what you say is based on facts, not opinions. Have a clear sense of your own sphere of responsibility, so you don't intrude on your boss' territory, and communicate with your boss—as often as you need to. A relationship based on trust and confidence means you don't waste her time, no matter how often you talk.

- **Be loyal**. "I had a boss who was not considered an easy guy to work for, but we got along fine. He just did things differently than other people. Because he knew I was loyal to him and what he wanted, we built a great relationship."

- **Understand your boss and her style**. "Do the best you can with that information. When you're not happy with your boss, your job can be pretty darn miserable. But when you are happy, it can be empowering and exciting."

## Keep Your Word

One rule for an *employee* to remember in managing his boss is to do things that remind your boss on a regular basis how valuable you are. For a *manager*, the first rule is to keep your word. Don't promise your boss or staff you are going to do things you only hope you are going to do. Make sure you are ready, willing, and able to do what you say you will.

Too many managers vaguely promise: "This is going to be a family-friendly office," and "We are going to improve communications around here," and then day-to-day operations prevent them from fulfilling those promises. They don't realize others remember what they say—even if they say it in an offhand way—and that failure to deliver compromises their stature as a leader.

If you say your office is going to be family-friendly, take actions to ensure it is, and let your decisions be guided by that promise. And don't let those promises fall by the wayside without explaining why.

When dealing with your own supervisor, keeping your word is even more important. A senior-level supervisor, or the owner of a company, expects you to carry out your assigned tasks with a minimum of supervision. If you are given an assignment, and you have some doubts about the ability of your staff to accomplish it, the time to say so is right up front. Once you've told your boss you can accomplish a task, move heaven and earth to do it.

If you've scheduled a meeting with your boss, don't attempt to postpone it. If you've promised a report will be completed by a certain date, get it done. And if you've told your boss you're going to effectively discipline an employee who's not performing up to expectations, do it. Don't underestimate how difficult it can be to consistently keep your word. Every manager faces distractions, interruptions, and issues beyond her control. But it can be done.

Nearly everyone knows at least one person who is known for keeping her word; for under-promising and over-delivering; for doing what she says will be done, every single time. Those are the people you want to model your behavior around. Only give your word when you know you can do what you say you will. Remember that your boss, your staff, and everyone else will measure you by whether you keep your word or not. Be the person you say you are, and make sure you are someone who can be counted on to do what you say. Nothing will influence, or impress, your boss more than this.

## Complement (Not Compliment) Your Boss

You cannot succeed in your work without the support of your boss—and your boss cannot succeed without your support, either. Each of you has already achieved some level of success in your careers, and you're therefore both likely to be much more set in your ways than the average new employee. It's hard to change the behaviors that brought you that success, but one of you may have to do so, and it's not likely to be your boss.

Why change? Well, because your boss, just like anyone else, has strengths and weaknesses. Some bosses may be good at negotiation, but bad at public speaking; great at handling unusual situations but poor at managing people day-to-day; strong on keeping the course steady, but unable to manage in times of change. You need to study your boss, find out what she does well or badly, and then provide the kind of support that meets those needs.

If your boss is the indecisive or hesitant type, be specific in your suggestions. If the information you get is vague, ask enough questions to be sure you know what is wanted before instructing your staff. If your staff is being overloaded with work, ask for help—and for prioritization.

> **Figure 12.1**
>
> ## Coping With Difficult Bosses
>
> Nearly everyone knows of the legendary incompetence of the pointy-haired boss in the comic strip *Dilbert*, who combines ignorance and rudeness with cheerfulness and obliviousness. And then there's Michael Scott on the television program *The Office*, who is very proud of the "World's Best Boss" coffee mug he bought for himself at the local gift store.
>
> But poor managers are everywhere. Many higher-level supervisors don't have the skills to manage others correctly. If your boss is one of those people, he probably isn't going to change. Despite those bad behaviors, your boss has managed to attain success, so he probably won't change his approach now.
>
> In her book *Dealing With Difficult People*, trainer Roberta Cava lists characteristics of bosses with poor supervisory skills (2006).
>
> **Interference**. Cava points out that there's a reason the chain of command in business exists: If you've got only partial control over the work your staff does, your effectiveness—and that of your group—is undermined. If your staff goes around you to get help from your boss, or if your boss goes around you to give work to your staff members directly, you've got to remind your boss of the boundaries. You are the one responsible for your staff's work, and you can't do your job properly if your staff is encouraged and supervised by someone else.
>
> **Poor Delegation**. If your boss is vague with instructions, fill in the details during direct discussions. If there's a change later, put things in writing and get them confirmed. Then, when your boss makes more changes, pull out the list and express confusion. After a couple of such discussions, Cava believes, your boss will get the idea.
>
> **Obsessive Perfectionism**. If your boss expects everything to go right, every time, make sure there's an understanding of how much is being asked of you and your staff. Remind the boss that your people will have to shift priorities from other work to meet the boss's expectations. Document your accomplishments, and those of your staff, so that you can defend them to others when there's a perfectionist who sees you as failing to live up to standards.
>
> **Poor Disciplinary Techniques**. If your boss belittles you in front of your staff, other bosses, or anyone, such behavior cannot be tolerated. The first time, tell the boss privately that you can accept criticism far better in private. After that, walk away if you can; show no emotion if you can't.
>
> **Taking Credit for Work You and Your Staff Have Done**. As Cava acknowledges, this is a tough line to draw. Many times a boss is representing your entire organization, and believes individual or group accomplishments should not be highlighted. If it happens repeatedly, however, remind your boss privately where the work came from; document what the staff has done; and look for chances to boost your staff and work daily.

You need to understand the external pressures on your boss, including how top management, the public, or sales figures are affecting priorities. Finally, you need to become aware of how your boss likes to get information. Is there a preference for emails and memos, face-to-face meetings, or phone calls? Is your boss a detail-oriented person, or is the big picture enough? Are her instructions abstract, or are you given a set of specific objectives and told to report back on a regular basis? Observe your boss carefully, and make decisions accordingly.

In a 2007 article in the *Harvard Business Review*, authors John J. Gabarro and John P. Kotter state: "It is not uncommon for a boss to need more information than a subordinate would naturally supply, or for a subordinate to think the boss knows more than he or she actually does. Effective managers recognize that they probably underestimate what their bosses need to know and make sure they find ways to keep them informed through processes that fit their styles."

Remember, just as your time is a limited resource, so is that of your boss. Every time you ask a question, it takes up some of that precious time, so be selective. Don't depend on your boss anticipating all your needs, however; part of being in sync is knowing what to ask and when.

## Fine-Tune Your Relationship

Make sure you know what's important to your boss, even if it seems trivial to you. Working until 10 p.m. the night before may have entitled you to come in late for next morning's 8 o'clock staff meeting, but your boss—alas—may not think so, so show up if you can. Even if you know you're smarter than your boss, and you believe you should have gotten his job, keep your mouth shut and personal complaints to yourself. As Art Hamerschlag said, loyalty is a critical aspect of forging a good relationship, and there's an added benefit: If you're known to be loyal to your boss, your subordinates will tend to be loyal to you.

If your boss doesn't hate meetings, try to meet one-on-one regularly to talk about yourself, your accomplishments, and your future. Just because you're a manager now doesn't mean you don't still have career goals. In fact, those goals have likely broadened, and you need to be sure your boss is aware of them.

Make sure your boss always knows what you're working on, and what you and your staff have accomplished. Don't hesitate to speak up about your accomplishments during meetings; copy your boss on any commendation or thank-you emails. Invite the boss to your staff meetings occasionally, for the opportunity to see you and your staff in action.

Everyone—even a high-level supervisor—has issues that annoy them. Whatever you do, don't push those buttons. Don't take it personally when a decision goes against you or if your boss is grouchy toward you occasionally. As your own supervisory responsibilities teach you, managers are under a great deal of pressure, and sometimes that pressure has to come out somewhere. Remember that actions and accomplishments speak louder than words.

Always be prepared and professional when meeting with your boss. Anticipate questions and responses, and propose next steps. Listen to the feedback you receive, and take it seriously, even if you're thinking: "The boss just doesn't understand my problems." Prepare especially hard for meetings with more senior levels of management, and don't be tongue-tied or inhibited in their presence. Be comfortable in the same shoes they once wore.

# CHAPTER 13

# FIND TIME TO THINK

"We cannot solve our problems with the same thinking
we used when we created them."

—*Albert Einstein*

---

### In This Chapter

- Why you need to find time to think.
- How to find time to think.

---

In chapter 10, managers learned to think clearly and strategically, and learned ways to apply those skills in their daily activities. But in a world of continual emails, Facebook updates, and hundreds of millions of tweets a day (in January 2009, 2 million tweets were sent every day; in 2010, the number was 65 million; by July 2011, it was past 200 million) who has time to do that kind of thinking? Is today's world moving faster than the speed of thought?

Google, one of the companies that helped define the modern information age, is working to slow things down for its employees. They encourage their engineers to take 20 percent of their time to work on projects that aren't necessarily in their job description. Among the projects coming out of that initiative have been Google News, Google Reader, Google Trends, and Google Maps.

Long before Google, 3M gave all of their employees a portion of their time to develop their own ideas (the Post-it® note was developed that way). Hallmark Cards routinely sends their artists, designers, stylists, writers, and photographers out of the office for walks to help them think creatively. And Hewlett-Packard's HP Labs also offers employees time to explore ideas that may never pay off.

Individuals, too, find unique ways to carve out thinking time. Anthony Principi, a former cabinet secretary, found time to think on his morning jog and over a morning cup of coffee with a trusted friend. Leonardo da Vinci kept a bed in his studio to rest and take naps sometimes. Da Vinci was once chided by a patron for napping when he was supposed to be working, and reportedly said, "If I don't do this, you don't get the work." And Gandhi would take entire days off to meditate about his life and actions.

Most companies, however, don't give people time off to think—especially managers. It's expensive and only works if a company is truly receptive to new ideas. Many people don't know how to handle the freedom to do whatever they want, within limits. But every successful manager needs to find time to strategize, to analyze information, to consider decisions, and to be creative. It may just be the most productive thing you do.

## Carve Out Thinking Time

Many people use early morning jogs and coffee not only for fitness and nutrition, but also to think about the day ahead. If you're going to use running time as thinking time, though, take along a recording device to capture your good ideas as they occur to you—otherwise they'll be lost. Similarly, if good ideas come to you in dreams or just before falling asleep, keep a pad by your bedside. Most busy executives cite airplanes as a place where they can work uninterruptedly, and some people recommend thinking while driving.

Just the act of putting a notepad next to your bed may stimulate your brain, subconsciously or otherwise. Some people place waterproof marker boards in the shower, because they get great ideas while showering. If you have to, get up half an hour earlier, or go to bed half an hour later, to make room for thinking time.

Try to avoid driving to work. Let someone else get you there so you're free to spend your time thinking. Walking a few miles to work is a great way to start the day. Ev used to enjoy crossing the Brooklyn Bridge on foot every morning and evening to get to and from work—and the views of the Manhattan skyline, the busy New York City waterfront, the other city bridges, and even his fellow pedestrians never failed to inspire him. If you have to drive, at least park at the far end of the employee lot, to gather your thoughts before starting your day.

If you prefer to think at your desk, clear some time on your schedule when you won't be distracted. For an hour every day, call a meeting—with yourself. Don't answer the phone, don't check your email, don't let your staff come in unless it's urgent, and use the time to think. Before you do this, keep a log of your time for a week and find which times are slowest in your day; those are the times to schedule your solo meetings. To make the best use of that time, plan ahead.

If you make to-do lists every morning, that's the time to prepare an agenda. Keep a journal of your thoughts and ideas, just as you would keep minutes of your meetings with others. Give yourself facts and information to concentrate on.

There's probably nothing more disruptive to continual thought than the constant ping of incoming emails. If possible, designate certain times of day to read them and respond, then let them accumulate the rest of the time. Stay off Facebook—talk to people instead.

Go through your emails in sequential order. If you skip around to the important ones, you'll never get to the others. Take an action immediately after reading an email. If you need to think before responding or deleting, keep the message open until you've decided what to do.

Lunch at your desk is not a good idea, either. Get out and see people; a change of scenery can get you out of a thinking rut. If you've got to eat at your desk, take a walk after you're finished eating. Walking aids digestion, keeps you fit, and clears the mind. Is there a park or garden nearby where you can sit for a while during or after lunch? If you're sitting at Starbucks with a coffee, leave your smartphone alone, and concentrate on the coffee. Your mind will relax, and you'll be able to think.

As a new manager, you may initially think break time is a bad thing—not good for productivity. No manager likes to be told the person they're looking for is on break—they'll think you are malingering. But short breaks during the day help the brain relax, and a relaxed brain is always far more productive than an overtaxed one.

Your computer and your smartphone have lots of ways to remind you about meetings, appointments, and other things you'd otherwise keep in your head. Use them so that you can clear that part of your brain for thinking instead of remembering. Blogger Michael Hyatt (2007) suggests making a "not-to-do" list: a list of all the things you're going to stop doing in order to make room for thinking.

## EXPERT TIP

For a judge, time to think is not a luxury—it's a necessity. For the **Hon. Efrain L. Alvarado**, administrative judge for criminal matters for New York State's 12th Judicial District in the Bronx, "the magic words are 'hold my calls.'" Here's how else he finds time to think:

- **Get your staff to help**. "I have to be available to my fellow judges and to other people when they need me. I can't be thought of as unapproachable. So I've trained my staff to raise the gate and lower the gate: to know which calls I have to take and which can wait, or can be redirected to someone else."

- **Train others to shoulder additional responsibility**. "When I hold meetings, I don't want to be the only problem solver in the room. I'll tell my staff what needs to be done, and ask them to think out of the box to find a way to do it."

- **Set aside time to think**. Justice Alvarado looks for the slowest times of the day to deliberate by himself. "If I'm writing a decision, and it's almost ready to go, I want to review what I've done in one sitting. Then, I ask my staff to screen my calls, and I get to work."

- **Think 'on background.'** "If I don't see a solution to a problem when I look at it the first time, I set it aside and wait a few hours. When I come back to it, the solution is often apparent, because I've been chewing on it while doing other things."

## Delegate Tasks

You can also clear time to think from your busy schedule by delegating some of your work to your staff, as Justice Alvarado does. Too many managers believe they can do things faster and better than the people they supervise, so it's not worth the time it takes to train others to do those tasks. If you have that attitude, you are not likely to succeed as a manager.

For one thing, employees who are not trusted by their bosses to do even simple tasks are aware of that lack of trust. They lose confidence in themselves, and their morale is low. When their help truly is needed, they do poor work as a result—and then managers complain about how closely they need to be supervised. It's a vicious cycle.

For another, what if it does take you a few days to teach someone to do a task well? Once those few days are over, you'll never have to do it again, freeing you to do work that others really can't do. And finally, even if it takes one of your staff members an hour to do work you can do in 30 minutes, consider this—at the rate you're paid, it still may be cost-effective for that staff member to do the work. The supervisory responsibilities you can't delegate cannot be allowed to slide, so you're just going to have to find time for those.

So how do you delegate properly? The first thing to do is realize that other people can do what you can do—and they may be able to do them faster and better, especially if you've hired good people. If that happens, don't worry—be happy.  The second is to create a list of everything you'd like off your plate in an ideal world. Once you've got the list on paper, figure out what you really can delegate to your staff—and, if possible, what you can eliminate altogether. Don't delegate anything that needs to be done right away or is absolutely critical to your, or your organization's, future. Then look at every member of your staff: their strengths and weaknesses; their special abilities; and which of them are less busy relative to their colleagues. Be careful about several things, however:

- Don't delegate work that your job description or your level of expertise requires you to do personally.

- Understand that while you might be giving one of your staff members a task, you are still responsible for maintaining control and seeing that the work gets done.

- Don't set people up to fail. Make sure they are actually able to do the task.

- Don't be a micromanager. Tell people what you want them to do, and what you want to see when they're done. If they can do it without you telling them exactly how, then get out of the way—but do set deadlines, and find a way to monitor their progress.

- Make sure that whoever you delegate work to understands the importance of the task to both of you, and to your organization. Don't forget to give your subordinates proper credit when they succeed. As the coach Bear Bryant said: "If anything goes bad, I did it. If anything goes semi-good, we did it. If anything goes really good, then you did it. That's all it takes to get people to win football games for you."

**Figure 13.1**

Andrew Carnegie on Delegation

Andrew Carnegie was one of the wealthiest men of the 19th century, an industrialist who made most of his money owning steel-making factories. He later became one of the nation's greatest philanthropists, giving away most of his fortune to build Carnegie Hall in New York and on other philanthropic ventures such as Carnegie Mellon University. He was a poor factory worker as a young man, but learned to delegate once he became a business owner. When A.B. Farquhar, a fellow businessman, tried to impress Carnegie by saying that he was always in his office by 7 a.m., Carnegie reportedly laughed and said:

*"You must be a lazy man if it takes you 10 hours to do a day's work. What I do is to get good men, and I never give them orders. My directions seldom go beyond suggestions. Here in the morning I get reports from them. Within an hour I have disposed of everything, sent out all of my suggestions, the day's work is done, and I am ready to go out and enjoy myself!"*

## Reduce Interruptions

It is, unfortunately, the fate of a manager to be interrupted regularly, by bosses and the people being supervised. One study conducted in 1992 suggested that on average, middle managers are interrupted 73 times a day, or once every eight minutes (Swenson, 1992). And this was before email, so the number must now be higher.

There are ways, however, to keep that number down. As a senior manager and former speechwriter, Ev was often asked to take on emergency writing assignments that absolutely had to be done right, and done quickly. In his desk, he kept a "Danger: Attack Writer at Work. Do Not Feed" sign, which he hung on his closed door while doing his writing assignment. It was not only a matter of getting the work done. The concentration he required for writing at that level was so great that if someone did stick their head in the door to ask him a question unrelated to what he was working on, he was unable to answer the question at that time. A closed door and a "Do Not Disturb" sign, used judiciously, is a good way not to be interrupted when you're doing something important.

To minimize staff interruptions, ask them to make appointments to see you whenever possible. It's a win-win; they organize their thoughts, and you think in an unhurried way. Hold regular staff meetings, and tell people to save their issues—if they can—for the meeting. And think about whether you empower staff members enough. If they can make their own decisions without checking back with you on every step, they won't bother you as often. Finally, prioritize answering your staff's emails as quickly as possible, so they don't have to grab you in person to get a response.

One stratagem that works to discourage visitors is to stand up when they walk into the room, and remain standing throughout the conversation, forcing them to stand as well. To facilitate this, leave your briefcase, laptop, or even your overcoat on the visitor's chair in your office, and don't offer to remove it. Tell people you've only got a couple of minutes to talk, and stick to it.

Don't position your desk so that people can see you head on. They will take that as an invitation to come in and chat. Instead, position your desk at a 90-degree angle to the door. Keep conversations short by reducing eye contact and glancing at your watch. If you are sitting, don't lean back in your chair, because that communicates you are relaxed and have time to chat.

You can also gain thinking time by booking a meeting room for a few hours, taking your laptop, and not telling anyone. You could go to the local coffee shop. If your company has a library, become a regular visitor, especially around lunchtime.

Finally, stop interrupting yourself. Don't go for aimless walks around the office. Limit your trips to the vending machine, and don't make impetuous decisions to check "just one thing" on the Internet, especially if what you're checking isn't work-related. Don't have chats with your co-workers, subordinates, or even your bosses, just for the fun of it.

To be a manager who thinks during the day, you should use these tools: carve out thinking time; delegate when you can; and reduce the number of interruptions in your day.

# CHAPTER 14

# GET THE MESSAGE

"No man ever listened himself out of a job."

—*President Calvin Coolidge*

## In This Chapter

- Why many of us don't listen well.
- Common barriers to effective listening.
- Benefits of avoiding listening pitfalls.
- Checklist to improve your listening skills.

## Lack of Formal Education

Most people accept that listening is a critically important element of communication. Yet a great many of us don't really listen very well. Most of our daily communication skills were gained from formal learning combined with experience. For writing, we apply grammar rules from grade school and basic structures from high school composition. For public speaking, we think back to a "Speech 101" course, and add to it any experience gained since then. But most of us don't have formal education or training in listening.

### EXPERT TIP

In the fiercely competitive world of paper sales, **Ronald K. Peterson** achieved remarkable success, which he credits to "using my ears more than my mouth." He said listening to customers in a focused, determined manner was the secret to becoming the top paper salesman in the history of the Ris Paper company, and to remaining a leading salesman in the industry in the northeast region of the country for more than a decade. He said that recognizing the reason for the problem often points the way to a solution.

## EXPERT TIP

**Tom Harvey** is a brilliant, engaging leader with genuine empathy for people, as well as our personal friend. He was the number two executive running the huge federal department serving veterans. Other VA headquarters staff members also commented that he was respected as a boss and counted as a friend. He had an extraordinary ability to connect with people at many different levels of the organization by listening. His listening ability:

- Brought him new, important information about the organization.
- Enhanced his understanding of information he already knew.
- Helped him do his job better.
- Helped others do their jobs better.
- Gained the appreciation of others.

---

**Figure 14.1**

### The HUA Paradigm

On U.S. Army bases around the world, you're likely to hear frequent repetitions of a forceful vocal sound, something between an elongated grunt and a deep, abbreviated yell, which might be phonetically spelled "Hoo-ah!"

There are a number of stories about the origin of HUA, and an even larger list of its possible uses. The expression is an acceptable—even preferable—way to say anything from "Yes, Sergeant," to "Roger, message received," to "Glad to meet you, welcome," to, well, anything and everything except "no."

The most popular connotation of HUA, however, succinctly expresses the essence of effective listening: "Heard, Understood, Acknowledged."

Listeners should recognize the value of doing what HUA connotes. They should recognize if they can *honestly* express HUA after listening.

---

## Easier Said Than Heard

Assuming reasonable hearing ability and language fluency, listening to someone speaking would seem to be a nearly automatic process. It's not. According to the book *Communicating at Work*, employees, on average, spend about a third of each working day listening to others in verbal communication (Alessandra and Hunsaker, 1993). Immediately after listening, they understand and retain only about half of what they hear; retention after 48 hours falls to about 25 percent. Not only is such poor listening a huge waste of time and opportunity for information transfer, it also has a negative effect on workplace relationships. Apparent lack of listener interest causes tension and lack of trust among the staff. Poor listening by one employee will often be echoed by others, leading to eventual unraveling of the entire communication process.

If we can hear and interpret the words spoken to us, why is there such a problem understanding and retaining those words? After careful assessment of our own weaknesses as listeners, and a thorough review of the literature available from resources such as the International Listening Association (http://www.listen.org/), we've assembled a list of common barriers to effective listening. It appears below, along with some observations about how these things affect many of us. Note that these stumbling blocks frequently overlap and feed on each other. For example, it's clear that if you begin a sequence of listening when you're lacking in motivation—only half listening—it's quite natural to be easily distracted and completely tune out. The barriers include:

- **Lack of motivation.** Listening is hard work. Especially in a modern era of multi-tasking and many available diversions, it's not unusual to find what someone's saying as not very interesting. It's not necessary to listen intently to everyone and everything. But when you decide something is important, you should make an affirmative decision that you want to listen to that particular person or presentation—and make the commitment to do so effectively.

- **Distraction.** Even if you've decided to listen intently, holding your attention on the speaker's words can be like a house trailer clinging to the lot in a tornado. The stimuli pulling at you can be external—a siren in the distance, music playing in the next office—or closer at hand, including the speaker's appearance. You find yourself looking at his clothes, or the shape of his nose, or wondering about an accent.

- **Speed difference.** There's a significant gap between the speed of speech and the speed of listener comprehension. The average person speaks 110 to 150 words per minute, while the average listener can process 300 words per minute with full comprehension. So about half the time you're listening, you can be thinking of something else. Ideally, you are also thinking about what you've heard and are working to provide feedback signals. But a less disciplined listener might indulge in other unrelated thoughts.

- **Emotional reaction.** Even listeners who are sharply focused on the speaker face pitfalls from within, in the form of their own reaction to something said. In such cases, the impediments to effective listening range from a mild thought digression, to more serious surges of strong emotions. The former situations are more common, including instances in which the speaker mentions a place or event that evokes, for the listener, a digression down memory lane—during which the speaker is completely tuned out.

- **One-upmanship.** Some listeners cannot resist the inclination to "one-up" or "me too" a story, and they will interrupt a speaker to tell their own tale. On occasion such weighing in by the listener may be appropriate. But if a speaker is relating a story to make a point, even thinking about one-up stories becomes a barrier to effective listening.

In some instances, just noting the problem suggests a solution to dealing with it. Some other tips also can be helpful. Figure 14.2 is an easy reference checklist to serve as an antidote to listening problems, based on general guidance from resources such as the International Listening Association, and following the specific advice of exceptional listeners like Ron Peterson and Tom Harvey. And, yes, we tried to listen carefully while they were giving us suggestions.

---

**Figure 14.2**

### Effective Listening Checklist

Once you've decided you really want to listen to a person or presentation, make a conscious commitment to do so actively. Take as many of the following steps as possible:

- Tune in to the speaker.
  - Eliminate or ignore external distractions—turn off phones, put away unrelated papers.
  - Concentrate on the speaker's words—don't get distracted by the speaker's appearance, accent, or unusual movements.
  - Watch for body language such as gestures and facial expressions, which will help you interpret the speaker's words.
- Keep your focus on the speaker.
  - Don't let your thoughts wander; stay tuned in by mentally paraphrasing what the speaker is saying.
  - If the speaker tells a story, don't try to one-up by telling a story of your own.
  - Don't interrupt with a question, except for short queries to clarify or further elicit completion of the speaker's comments.
- Provide feedback.
  - Establish and maintain a pattern of eye contact with the speaker.
  - Nod your head, and provide other means of affirmation (if in private conversation, with brief comments).
  - When the speaker has finished or is at a break point, ask questions summarizing what you have heard.

---

# MANAGE YOUR MEETINGS

"A meeting is an interaction where the unwilling,
selected from the uninformed, led by the unsuitable,
to discuss the unnecessary, are required to write
a report on the unimportant."

—*T.A. Kayser*

---

### In This Chapter

- Why should we have meetings?
- Preparation for meetings is key.
- Best practices for planning, chairing,
  and participating.
- Make your meetings better.
- How to run remote meetings.

---

When thinking of meetings in the workplace, most people don't have great memories. Most of us are too familiar with tedious, unfocused, time-wasting, energy-sapping gatherings. We wade through monotonous minutiae, dealing with issues on which most attendees make no meaningful contribution. Useless and annoying meetings lead to countless jokes and cartoons.

Meetings also have positive features. The primary alternative to meetings—getting information on paper or in digital form—has limitations. As mentioned in chapter 7, people are influenced far more by a speaker's appearance and the sound of her voice than by the actual words spoken. No matter how advanced our high-tech communication becomes, there will always be times when live, interpersonal dynamics and nonverbal nuances of human communication justify physical gatherings.

Meetings are a good tool, but one that frequently isn't used very well. Many leave us feeling like they were a total waste of time, but sometimes we leave feeling energized, with a sense that we really accomplished something. There are reasons for these mixed experiences, but it's very worthwhile for managers to be positive about meetings. You should embrace meetings for the opportunities they bring.

# For New Managers

In many cases, meetings give upwardly mobile men and women their most visible opportunities to demonstrate proficiency in intellect, business acumen, language fluency, leadership ability, and social skills. Meetings bring chances for new managers to interact with people at several levels; participating effectively has obvious career-enhancing implications.

Having observed some of the good and bad about meetings, we might wonder, what's the worst case scenario? That would be when lack of preparation and poor meeting management are combined with apathetic and inept participation by attendees. Managers can avoid such ugly outcomes by effectively planning, chairing, and facilitating; attendees can do their part by actively participating. This chapter will broaden our look at meetings, from those regular staff get-togethers, to the more formal variety, where attendees might include people from outside and inside an organization. There are some differences between informal staff gatherings and more prescribed meetings, in both planning and in conducting them. But there are many similarities, and the keys to running and participating in them efficiently are much the same. These key steps are detailed, with additional tips and three checklists to make the process user-friendly. We'll focus on the type of meetings most of you will encounter: The number of attendees is large enough for group dynamics, but small enough to allow reaching consensus and decisions.

## Is a Meeting Necessary?

When you add up the cost of everyone's time—not just the minutes getting and sitting there, but interrupting other work, plus travel costs, meeting-room and support expenses—meetings become an expensive proposition.

If the goal is to share information, the same purpose might be accomplished via an email message with attachments, or through posting the information at a common access website with notification to everyone concerned. Even if feedback on the new information is desired, similar "meetingless" approaches can be used. You can request comments in email responses or via postings in an organization's electronic message board. In an increasingly busy work environment, such methods are replacing traditional meetings more often. Some organizations conduct virtually all of their business—including voting on issues—electronically, without a single, in-person meeting ever taking place.

Decide whether what you need to accomplish requires the effort and expense of a meeting. If your purpose goes beyond simple distribution and single-layered response, a meeting may be needed. Decide if you have any of the following requirements:

- Sharing information in a way that allows dynamic interaction.
- Developing ideas and solutions that require the combined knowledge and skills of more than one individual.
- Motivating staff, and publicly acknowledging achievements.
- Negotiating differences among conflicting ideas and forging consensus.

Once you've determined that one or more of these requirements exist, are you ready to round up the usual suspects, and just head into the conference room? Not exactly. Launching into a meeting without adequate prep work is a recipe for unfocused, chaotic interaction with an unpredictable outcome.

## Case History: Impromptu Meeting to Solve Problems

**Scenario:** *An evolving situation at the Tru-Glow Energy Company forces the boss to call an impromptu meeting. Information he needs to understand and resolve the problem is fragmented among three groups:*

- *Some customers have come to complain that Tru-Glow is not meeting expectations to provide clean-energy heating and cooling.*

- *The Tru-Glow sales team is calling these customers unreasonable and is also reporting that the company's engineers are not responsive.*

- *Tru-Glow production engineers are calling the sales team idiots and the customers overly pampered.*

*Inviting the customers and division chiefs into the conference room, the boss makes cursory introductions. The customers are a grocer specializing in organic fruits and vegetables (Wholesome Vegemart), and the owner of an organic nursery (Everbloom Greenhouse), who sells plants and floral arrangements "produced in a sustainable environment."*

*Paraphrasing a bit in an attempt to calm down the volatile tone, the boss summarizes the customers' complaints. While both had contracted for Tru-Glow's innovative heating and cooling systems because of their commitment to clean, nonpolluting energy, they've been "a bit dissatisfied at times because of uneven temperature levels and questions about air quality."*

*At this point, the manager of Wholesome Vegemart interrupts to say, "Uneven temperature is an understatement; some days your ridiculously expensive system can't get within 10 degrees of a comfortable level—too cold in winter, too hot in summer—"*

*Tru-Glow's sales manager cuts him off: "Look, you know your system depends on wind turbines and solar power. On cloudy days with no wind, those primary generators aren't working. That's what makes Tru-Glow's energy system so unique; our auxiliary system is the only noncarbon-based backup technology in existence. You just hit that auxiliary power button a few times, and the temperature will gradually even out."*

*That's when the owner of Everbloom Greenhouse loses it: "Gradually doesn't work for us," she says. "We can't have our customers freezing in winter and soaked with sweat in summer. I push that auxiliary power button again and again, but it takes a long time for the temperature to come around. And that's when the air quality tanks. My greenhouse fills up with indoor smog, with visible, black airborne particles."*

*The perplexed look on the sales chief's face suggests he's never heard of this phenomenon, and he does his best to sound surprised: "That's strange; sounds like a system calibration problem. The engineers should be able to work that out with a few adjustments—"*

*That's as far as he gets, what with the engineering chief on his feet, waving his hands and saying, "No, no, no! We've said, repeatedly, that the auxiliary can only be triggered once every hour. You sales guys know the backup is a subsoil heat extractor. Pushing that auxiliary button repeatedly will cause excessive air injection into the soil, stirring dirt into the airflow. That indoor smog is a plain old cloud of dirt in the air."*

*Things degenerate into everyone yelling at once, as the boss considers saying that the meeting is getting off track. But he realizes that with no announced purpose or agenda, it never really had a track. There's no doubt, however, the meeting is out of control—not advancing toward a resolution and increasing, rather than easing, animosities among participants. The meeting dissolves as the customers storm out, leaving the sales and engineering teams arguing with each other.*

Would better management during the Tru-Glow meeting have made a difference? For example, would the outcome have been different if the boss had been more persuasive in articulating the company's commitment to customer service? Or might he have smoothed things over with a more temperate restatement of the engineer's disturbing comments? Perhaps this would have helped a bit, but not a great deal would have changed. By the time this meeting started, it was too late.

## Build a Solid Foundation

A good paint job can only be achieved if the base preparation work is done well; rough spots must be sanded smooth and primer applied evenly. No matter how good the quality of the paint, no matter how skilled the person spraying the color coats—bad prep job equals bad finish. A meeting is like a paint job; to achieve a decent end result, the prep work has to be done well.

For any meeting, prep work begins with determining and clearly spelling out the purpose. Next comes the selection of agenda items, which anticipate outcomes that will accomplish the meeting's stated purpose. If such prep work had taken place at Tru-Glow, the purpose might have been stated in this way: "To hear concerns about Tru-Glow heating and cooling systems, ascertain reasons for problems, determine whether system information or technical adjustments are needed, and ultimately assure customer satisfaction."

In the course of working up that statement of the meeting's purpose, some preliminary inquiries of the customer would have helped the company recognize the essence of the problem. In developing the agenda items, it's reasonable to expect that the company would be fully prepared to describe the limitations of such environmentally sensitive equipment, and able to explore solutions, such as turning on the auxiliary unit earlier, but triggering it less frequently. This type of advance work clearly would have led to a meeting with a more acceptable outcome for both customers and the company.

For any meeting, once the purpose and agenda items have been determined, it's time to decide who should attend. This, too, should be carefully planned. Some might think the more the merrier, but that's problematic for several reasons. First, it ignores the matter of expense; every person in the meeting who cannot contribute to the process represents a direct waste of resources. Second, experience shows that decision-making ability at meetings is inversely proportional to the number of attendees—the more people at a meeting, the less chance there is to reach agreement and take action. For most meetings, it's advisable to restrict invitations to those who can contribute to accomplishing the meeting's purpose.

With preliminary decisions made, schedules can be checked, and a date, time, and place for the meeting can be set. These steps seem pretty straightforward, but professional planners often use some special techniques to help them set up successful meetings.

**EXPERT TIP**

As president of the Healthcare Leadership Council, Mary Grealy arranges exceptionally high-level meetings. Her organization is a coalition of chief executives from several disciplines in American healthcare, including academic health centers, hospitals, health plans, medical-device manufacturers, and pharmaceutical companies. With such an elite membership, HLC meetings need to be models of efficiency. Grealy provides these tips for avoiding pitfalls, making sure your meeting has the right agenda, and getting off to a running start:

- **Start with a firm idea of the meeting's purpose.** But keep the agenda in draft form until you consult with key participants on specific agenda items and desired outcomes.

- **Seek advice on who has special insight about the issues.** During pre-meeting calls to define agenda items, ask those persons "in the know" to be discussion leaders. When the meeting actually begins, you'll have good confidence that the agenda is germane and a head start on the work of the meeting, because key members already are tuned in.

- **Use best practice checklists.** This makes sure you don't overlook important details. We use one for planning a meeting (Figure 15.1) and one for chairing a meeting (Figure 15.2).

## Best Practices for Planning, Chairing, and Participating

Such sophisticated advance work is not practical for every meeting, especially the numerous, lower- and mid-level confabs that happen every day. But knowing the optimal way to proceed is useful, and can pay off nicely on occasion, when we do need to plan for a particularly important meeting. So there are a couple of best practice checklists: one for planning a meeting (Figure 15.1) and one for chairing a meeting (Figure 15.2).

Most new managers are attendees at lots of meetings, but don't get called on very frequently to chair them. So meeting etiquette from the standpoint of participants is important: how to contribute in a meaningful way, and be perceived as astute, judicious, and a team player. Figure 15.3 is a checklist of tips for participating at meetings.

## Slay the Draggin'

Meetings that drag on are universally dreaded. The sluggish meeting has stubbornly resisted the modern world's trend toward a faster pace the way the cockroach has resisted evolution. Why? There are several proposed reasons: meetings provide a social opportunity to escape; people are basically undisciplined; people like to hear themselves talk; people can't agree.

**Figure 15.1**

### Checklist for Meeting Planning

1. Determine and spell out purpose.

2. Initially consider agenda items and attendees.

3. Consult with stakeholders to refine agenda items and select attendees.

4. Finalize agenda items, set discussion and start times for each, and briefly state desired outcomes.

5. Set date and time (after coordinating schedule with key attendees).

6. Assign duties: notetaker, facilitator/presenter for specific agenda items, timekeeper.

7. Select appropriate background materials, in consultation with key participants.

8. Send out meeting notice, in accordance with any required formal notifications.

9. Send out agenda (may also serve as meeting notice, if other formal notice is not required) and background materials. For major meetings, this information should be available to participants at least three days in advance. This transmission also should inquire whether any attendees will have special accessibility needs at the meeting.

10. Send out meeting reminder 24 hours in advance.

These are all provocative answers. But the real reason meetings drag on is because they can. The people who run meetings allow it, by not serving notice that we care about time. The solution, therefore, is to strongly make the point—in several ways—that we *do* care about time, and we're going to treat it as a precious commodity throughout the meeting process.

For expediting meetings, first, start on time. Second, list the start discussion time of each agenda item and stick to it. Strict adherence to a schedule sends a message—one that most people will support.

It's a very common failing to start meetings a few minutes late. It's customary for greetings and small talk as people arrive; a pleasant interlude in our culture that establishes a cordial atmosphere. When this chitchat runs past the published start time of a meeting, it also sends a signal—that time is not of the essence. Knowing meetings often have such a soft start time, people may drift in a few minutes late, since they won't miss anything. And once everyone is there, when the meeting is belatedly called to order, people then won't discipline their comments. The feeling of leisure time persists.

If you're the chair, a good plan for launching a smooth and sharp meeting begins by arriving at the location at least 15 minutes early. This way, you can participate in the unofficial, but important, pleasantries of greetings and small talk. Then, at precisely the appointed time, call the meeting to order. Don't be delayed by the absence of a few people, or even by someone's comments that "so-and-so is just out in the hallway, on their way in." Start the meeting with a welcome, and your preliminary comments about the purpose of the meeting.

**Figure 15.2**

## Checklist for Chairing: Day of the Meeting

1. Arrive early (handle unforeseen logistical details, engage in small talk).

2. Start on time.

   - Curtail small talk precisely at posted time to begin meeting.
   - Officially launch meeting exactly on time, even if several participants are late (they can catch up via minutes or be brought up to speed by word of mouth later).

3. Articulate purpose of the meeting and set ground rules.

   - Ask for muting of phone/text messaging.
   - State intention to start discussion of each agenda item on time, so that overall meeting will end on time.
   - Note who will be taking minutes, and who will help keep time.

4. Announce items on the agenda with names of facilitators or presenters.

5. Encourage participation by everyone.

   - Seek to compliment all contributions as helpful.
   - The Chair should avoid taking a strong position on an item until discussion on that item is concluded.

6. Assert ground rules.

   - Maintain focus on agenda; use "parking lot" of flipchart or whiteboard to note off-topic points for later review. After the meeting, review those points and follow up later with all participants.
   - Follow Robert's Rules of Order (see Figure 15.4) in considering motions, taking votes, and other proceedings (unless organization is otherwise bound by law to some other rules).
   - Do not permit personal criticism; dissuade interruption of speakers.

7. Close out each agenda item at specified time.

   - Monitor the time during discussion. If progress is slow, remind participants there is limited time to reach resolution. In instances where discussion has been thorough, ask if anyone might call the question, move to vote, or otherwise take action. If not, note that this item may need further study and later resolution.
   - A couple minutes before time expires on each item, announce that it's time to resolve this item or move it over for future consideration.

8. Fix responsibilities for each action item.

   - Summarize decision or other action for each item.
   - Note who has responsibility for each item, along with the timetable for any next steps.

9. Finish overall meeting on time.

**Figure 15.3**

Checklist for Meeting Participants

*Before the Meeting*

1. Review agenda, consider relevant issues to you, and points you may wish to raise during the meeting. **If the meeting is not relevant to you and you don't see how you can benefit or contribute, question whether your presence is really necessary.**

2. Read background materials.

3. Have a general understanding of the basics of Robert's Rules of Order (see Figure 15.4), and especially know the procedure for offering and amending motions.

*Day of the Meeting*

1. Arrive early (engage in small talk; be ready to start on time).

2. If meeting does not have formal name tags at seats, make an informal seating chart in your notes, to help you recall names and positions.

3. Mute your phone/text messaging devices.

4. Don't hesitate to speak up when you have something to ask or add. You have to show you are a sharp, engaged team player in a courteous manner:

   - Be concise and precise.
   - Don't interrupt other speakers.
   - It's OK to challenge other viewpoints, but don't be contentious.
   - Stay focused on the agenda item being discussed.

5. If any action items are assigned to you, note exact details of what's expected, and the timeline.

The impact of your on-time start will resonate in this meeting, and echo onto future meetings in your charge. Don't repeat yourself as latecomers arrive; they usually can catch up fairly quickly, or get updated by word of mouth during break time. If they're significantly late, they can read the minutes afterward.

Start the meeting by stating the purpose, which should also be printed on the agenda, and briefly cite the agenda items. Emphasize your intention to end the meeting on time.

In many cases, this type of meeting launch will be all you need to establish the importance of time; the sense of urgency in keeping things moving is usually contagious. If you gently keep things on track, prodding here and there to prompt things toward closure through votes or other action, and start each new agenda item on time, you'll have a good chance for a tight and tidy meeting.

Sometimes, however, more drastic measures are needed to expedite meetings. For example, let's say you've learned at your regular monthly meetings that several of the attendees never bother to read the background materials. These folks want to waste long periods of time during meetings chatting about history and debating facts explained in those documents they might have studied in advance. You can sometimes head off such behavior when sending out the agenda and background materials, by adding a cover note stating: "Please review this material in advance. The schedule set for each agenda item and its discussion will be strictly adhered to." The good team players will get the message; the incorrigible ones must be worked around.

Then, of course, there's the problem of long-winded participants. If you've already followed the above suggested tips to serve notice about the essence of time, and they're still droning on, you're faced with two options: the "soft signal" to wrap up—typically appropriate when the windbag is your boss or otherwise senior to you—or the "hard-plug pull," which is much more satisfying.

Soft-signal wording could be: "I hate to interrupt, because Mr. Prattler certainly is putting this issue into perspective in a very compelling way. But our agenda time has run out, and I'm wondering if we can resolve this with some action now, or if we should hold it for a discussion at a later time?" Play it by ear at that point; try to move on to the next item, but hey—keeping your job is more important than an on-time meeting.

---

**Figure 15.4**

Robert's Rules of Order

*Who was Robert, and how come he gets to set the rules?*

During the United States Civil War, U.S. Army Brigadier General Henry Robert was asked to preside over a church meeting in New Bedford, Mass. By his own account, his lack of knowledge about how to run such an event made for a very unsatisfactory occasion.

The General then researched common guidance on running meetings, but found only conflicting ideas. He therefore wrote his own manual of parliamentary procedures for organizations, published in 1876 as *Robert's Rules of Order*. His rules are loosely based on procedures followed in the U.S. House of Representatives, modified to fit more common circumstances in social meetings.

*Robert's Rules of Order* is not legally binding, but is widely accepted as the official guide for running meetings. In fact, the copyright expired on the original *Robert's Rules* many years ago, and there are now versions in the public domain. You can read up on the rules and reference them for free at several websites. Two of those with excellent search and reference capabilities are *www.rulesonline.com* and *www.robertsrules.org*.

It's a good investment for new managers to buy a hard copy of the rules in brief. This is an abbreviated, user-friendly version of the official 2011 edition rules.

The 208-page book's official title is *Robert's Rules of Order Newly Revised In Brief, 2nd edition.*

Who wouldn't prefer the hard-plug pull? For example, you hold up your hand to cut off the blabbermouth in mid-sentence, and say something like, "In the interest of our very limited time, I want to remind everyone we can only move on by talking about future solutions. Would anyone like to make a motion at this time (if you're using Robert's Rules), or do we need to schedule this item for future consideration?"

There are more extreme suggestions to keep meetings short, including riveting attention on the time by using prominent clocks or timers with audible alarms. Another approach is to have everyone stand during the entire meeting, which eliminates participants getting overly comfortable. One unique idea is to furnish participants with extensive liquid refreshment, with the stated rule that the meeting is over when the first person gets up to use the restroom.

For formal business meetings with attendees from outside your organization, we don't recommend such methods. But if your regular internal meetings are seriously bogging down and you've not had success with gentler, kinder techniques, more extreme measures to speed things up might be worth a try.

## Remote Meetings: Conference Calls, Webinars, and Teleconferences

From simple telephone conference calls to sophisticated teleconferences, the several levels of remotely attended meetings have some things in common:

- They allow some degree of participation without being physically present, saving the time and expense of travel.
- They exchange ease of participation for some loss of sensory information (inability or reduced ability to see other participants).
- Without immediate visual cues to help in "speaker traffic control," a common problem of remote meetings is "simul-talk"—the tendency of more than one person to start talking at the same time.
- The open-architecture nature of these meetings makes them especially vulnerable to accidental noise, such as inadvertently activated hold music, barking dogs, and bathroom sounds.
- Video imaging of other participants does not allow for direct eye contact.
- And most importantly, in order to be effective, they all still require the same premeeting preparations: development of a structured agenda and advanced distribution of discussion materials.

The basic conference call—involving telephone participation by some or all attendees—has been a regular meeting technique for several years. This type of easy-to-set-up meeting requires the least equipment: a decent telephone handset. However, the conference-call meeting is the most difficult to keep on track, because the lack of any visual contact interferes with getting and keeping the attention of attendees.

If you want to conduct conference-call meetings, and your company doesn't have a telephone or IT support team to guide you, some quick research on the Internet should lead you to a conference-call provider with the right blend of cost and services. You will have to make choices such as whether you want to pay one overall bill per call, or have the participants billed for their time on the line, and whether you want the call recorded for playback.

The next step up from the conference call—the webinar—is more complex and provides more meeting involvement. This step adds a visual dimension to the audio connection in a remote meeting, typically allowing a presenter to share digital slide presentations, webpages, or other multimedia content with participants. Most webinar arrangements allow participants to interact with the presenter by asking questions or expressing opinions in real time through instant messaging or email.

The choice of a company to provide webinar setup and regular service is an important one, dictating whether you will pay for services on a per-webinar basis, or through a monthly fee. It's easy to learn how to set up a webinar by checking out sites on the Internet that rate these services and provide a matrix to compare what they offer with their prices.

A final level of complexity in the remote meeting is the teleconference or web conference—in which more than one site transmits live audio and video tracks. Teleconferences are normally limited to about six participants, all of whom have the webcams, microphones, and special routing equipment needed to send and receive audio and video tracks. Participants typically see a boxed image of each of the other participants on their monitors. This type of digitally transmitted meeting, although somewhat intensive in equipment and limited in size, most closely resembles live meetings, in terms of participants' ability to interact. Again, if your company or organization does not have a large IT support team, you can get plenty of information by doing an Internet search on top 10 ratings for teleconferences.

With all the exotic capabilities of webinars and web conferences, and the ever-growing cost and travel time constraints of face-to-face meetings, why haven't these digitally enhanced remote meetings completely taken over? Here are some reasons:

- **Perception of high cost.** When teleconferences were first available, the technology was expensive. As costs have dramatically dropped, the perception of high cost has lagged a bit. Attitudes will continue to evolve and the process will become more popular as prices keep dropping.

- **User-unfriendliness.** Nontechnical people are intimidated by the complexity of the teleconference process. Any time a minor glitch results from a poor connection or an unplugged cord—in the absence of a talented IT support team—many small organizations will turn back to conventional meetings.

- **Self-consciousness about being on camera.** Some people are not enamored with their appearance on camera, and many others are simply uncomfortable about being on camera.

- **No direct eye contact.** Even when all participants appear via video, and systems work properly, studies have shown that people react negatively to having no direct eye contact.

So remote meeting alternatives are growing in functionality and popularity, but they're not about to supplant conventional meetings just yet. If they do, managers can successfully participate in them through following the same approaches for all meetings.

**CHAPTER 16**

# INTERVIEW PROSPECTIVE EMPLOYEES

"Your attitude, not your aptitude,
will determine your altitude."

—*Zig Ziglar*

---

### In This Chapter

- Focus exclusively on the key dynamic of the manager meeting with and talking to the applicant.

---

Job interviews are so nerve-racking that they've become the subject of humorous skits and parodies. The spoofs go to extremes in portraying awkward applicants struggling with outrageous interview questions. Part of what makes the subject so funny is the truth within the satire: Interviewing can be stressful on either side of the desk.

A lot is riding on the interview process; for one party, it's a gateway to employment and compensation, with all the implications of self-reliance and societal standing. For the other party, it represents a vital opportunity to cut through abstract written information on applications and résumés to identify a valuable employee—the lifeblood of any organization.

---

**Reminder 16.1**

Hiring Activities in Organizations

- Classify jobs.
- Develop position descriptions.
- Advertise vacancies.
- Arrange interviews.
- Interview prospective employees. (By manager.)
- Check job references.

Mostly these will be handled by HR, but if you have a smaller company, sometimes managers have to handle these tasks.

---

**EXPERT TIP**

**Robert Baugh,** who served for several years as director of human resources at Mitsubishi Polyester Films America, and chairman of the global HR committee for Mitsubishi Films Group, says hiring interviews are extremely important.

**Amy Goldstein**, Mid-Atlantic HR director at Marriott International, also cautions against undue haste in the interview process.

They both suggest taking care in the interview process, and emphasize asking specific questions during the interview, and some concluding open-ended questions. They also agree that the behavioral event interview is the most successful. They point to three elements in favor of this approach:

- **It grew out of research by psychologists**, who found that traditional academic exams and IQ tests were not good predictors of job effectiveness.

- **Studies have shown that work competence is effectively indicated** by having interviewees relate past instances in which they demonstrated specific job skills.

- **It's a very flexible approach**; you can tailor behavioral questions to any occupation, and then evaluate the responses at various levels of sophistication.

## Interview Guidance

Here is a generic agenda to guide a manager through a typical interview (see Figure 16.1).

Some interview questions could lead to legal problems. We'll examine the reasons and provide a checklist for those precautions—including reference to the underlying practices that are prohibited by various federal, state, and municipal laws. (See Figure 16.2.)

## Follow the Road Map

"Freelancing" is the term Robert Baugh uses to describe the way some managers go into interviews without a plan, figuring to just chat with applicants—"get to know them" —relying on pure intuition and knowledge of human nature to determine suitability for a job. It's a bad idea to approach interviews without a plan. Here's why:

- With no road map, the discussion is likely to spin off in any direction—usually in ways not helpful to determining the applicants' capabilities.

- Having no list of questions or subjects—not even a mental one—means little chance that you will ask each applicant the same question in the same way.

- Free-form discussion may consume so much time and energy that the most important things to discuss, such as applicable knowledge and skills related to the job, may be left out or insufficiently covered.

- Congeniality during an unfocused interview based on matters not related to the job—reminiscing about a school both attended, or talking about shared interest in some sport or hobby—can lead to highly subjective judgments about applicants' suitability for a job.

---

**Figure 16.1**

Agenda for Interview

10:00 a.m.
    **Welcome**

- Small talk to put applicant at ease.
- Confirm understanding (job announcement number XYZ ; salary level XX).

10:05 a.m.
    **Discuss applicant's résumé.**

- Educational background.
- Work history—clarify questions in job descriptions.

10:15 a.m.
    **Applicant's short-term objectives and career goals.**

10:20 a.m.
    **Describe some elements of the position.**

- Technical knowledge and skills needed.
- Leadership abilities required.

10:25 a.m.
    **Questions (separate list) to determine applicant competencies:**

- Describe situations demonstrating technical knowledge and skills.
- Describe leadership experiences in previous jobs.

10:40 a.m.
    **Tell applicant about company history and culture.**

10:43 a.m.
    **Ask if applicant has any questions.**

10:45 a.m.
    **Thank applicant/conclude interview.**

---

Experts agree interviews should have proper agendas like other business meetings. An ending time should be planned, but it shouldn't appear in print; either party could end the interview early if it is not a good fit, and there's no reason to waste more time.

## Figure 16.2

### Interview Questions to Avoid

To avoid discrimination based on religious affiliation, don't ask:

- What religion do you practice?
- Do you observe any religious holidays?
- Do you belong to any clubs or social organizations?

To avoid discrimination based on nationality, don't ask:

- Are you a U.S. citizen? (OK to ask, and should ask: Can you legally work in the U.S.?)
- What's your first language?

To avoid discrimination based on age, don't ask:

- How old are you?
- Will you work much longer before retiring?

To avoid discrimination based on marital and family status, don't ask:

- Are you married? Is this your maiden name?
- Do you have any kids? Do you plan on having children?
- Are you pregnant?
- Who is your closest relative to notify in case of an emergency? (OK to ask who to notify, just not if this person is a relative.)

To avoid discrimination based on health, don't ask:

- Do you smoke or drink?

- Do you take drugs? (Improper to ask about prescription drugs, but may ask if applicant takes illegal drugs. However, the small likelihood of a straight answer suggests just leaving this out.)
- How much do you weigh?
- How tall are you?
- How many days were you out sick last year? (OK to ask how many scheduled days of work did you miss?—without saying due to sickness.)
- Do you have any disabilities?
- Have you had any recent illnesses or operations?

To avoid discrimination based on military service, don't ask:

- Were you honorably discharged from the U.S. Armed Forces?
- Are you a member of the Reserves or the National Guard?

To avoid discrimination based on legal history, don't ask:

- Have you ever been arrested? (OK to ask have you ever been convicted of a specific crime?—if related to type of work applied for. For example: convicted of fraud if working in accounting or banking.)

Don't show the complete agenda to the applicant; it may include items like, "Start out with small talk to put interviewee at ease." But the interviewer might give the applicant an informal preview of the agenda (shown in Figure 16.1), along the following lines:

- *Let me just tell you how the process works here:*
  - *First, we should confirm we're on the same page, talking about job announcement number XYZ—which is a level XX supervisory position, with a salary range from $x to $xx.*

○ *We'll start with you telling me a bit about your educational qualifications and work history.*

○ *Then, I'll describe some elements of the job here, and we can talk about whether your abilities and past experiences might help you fit into those kinds of tasks.*

○ *Along the way, we should talk about your short-term objectives and career goals.*

○ *Next, I'll tell you a little bit about the company, our culture, and our employee family, so you'll have a better feel for us.*

○ *Finally, I'll see if you want to tell me anything else about your qualifications for this position, and see if you have any questions for me—about the job or the company.*

## Avoid the Elephant in the Room

In the course of any interview, there's an overwhelming presence everyone is aware of, but no one readily talks about. This is discrimination in hiring based on race, gender, age, religion, national origin, pregnancy, or parenting status.

Few people know all the details, but most folks know there are laws against discrimination in hiring. Before talking about specific restrictions, let's take a minute to examine how discrimination happens. An understanding of this, and an appreciation for the value of diversity in business, can take us a long way toward avoiding discrimination.

There's no denying there are wrong-thinking people in the world: racism, chauvinism, xenophobia, and disrespect for the elderly clearly underlie discrimination throughout society, including all aspects of employment. But it's accurate to say a significant amount of discrimination in hiring is unintentional. It's a simple fact of human nature that we feel comfortable with people like ourselves.

When an interviewer and applicant are similar in appearance, went to the same schools, came from the same kind of neighborhood, or shared other things in their backgrounds, then some degree of affinity is inevitable. This is especially true when the hiring process is affected by interviewers who place a lot of importance on subjective feelings, or how they hit it off with certain applicants. So conducting interviews in an orderly fashion, asking the same questions of every applicant, and considering answers objectively, is the first line of defense against inadvertent discrimination.

Aside from legal considerations, making hiring judgments based on affinity is bad business. The human nature inclination to associate with people like yourself—if allowed to influence hiring decisions—tends to produce the opposite of diversity: a homogeneous workforce. In organizations where people are alike, there are serious weaknesses. People tend to think and act alike, and there is an absence of fresh thinking, a loss of creativity, and a lack of flexibility.

In the emerging global marketplace, a diverse workforce has significantly greater ability to identify and understand needs, and fits in more easily in working with other cultures to meet those needs.

Research confirms the value of diversity. Several studies show this, prominently one by Louisiana Tech University examining the performance of firms in the banking industry with different levels of diversity. This study found greater diversity provided a competitive advantage in productivity, return on equity, and market performance (Richard, 2000).

## Letter of the Law on Discrimination

There are hundreds of federal, state, and local laws related to the hiring process. There are too many to list or to provide details about, but a few of these laws are central to discrimination in hiring.

- Title VII of the Civil Rights Act of 1964 prohibits employment discrimination based on race, color, religion, gender, or national origin.
- The Age Discrimination in Employment Act of 1967 prohibits discrimination against persons age 40 and older.
- The Rehabilitation Act of 1973 and the Americans with Disabilities Act of 1990 combine to prohibit discrimination against persons with disabilities.
- The Pregnancy Discrimination Act of 1978 prohibits discrimination on the basis of pregnancy or childbirth.

In general, these laws apply to all private employers, state and local governments, and educational institutions that employ at least 15 workers. Similar prohibitions against discrimination in federal agencies are set forth in the Code of Federal Regulations (CFR) and are reinforced in the Civil Service Reform Act of 1978.

As noted above, in organizations large enough to have such staff support, HR professionals should be knowledgeable about state and local laws governing employment, and they can provide any additional guidance needed to avoid actual or perceived discrimination. Smaller organizations without professional HR support in hiring should make sure local statutes are not more stringent than the federal laws mentioned here. A good place to start is with the department of labor for your individual state; links to the individual state websites can be found at: *http://www.statelocalgov.net/50states-jobs.cfm*.

In view of the many laws in place against discrimination in hiring, should managers be nervous about asking questions in interviews? No, they should be cautious, and take care with the questions they ask and how they evaluate the answers.

Mitsubishi's Robert Baugh explains that "It's not actually illegal to ask any particular question during an interview; what's illegal is if certain questions are asked, and the answers are then used to discriminate."

Some questions so directly establish a basis for discrimination it's obvious they are inappropriate. Examples: "That's an interesting accent; where were you born?" (leads to discrimination based on national origin); and, "Your résumé shows you've really been around—how old are you?" (leads to discrimination based on age).

Other questions are less obvious in setting the stage for trouble. For example, something like the following might seem simply conversational: "We're a very socially friendly company and like for our employees to be involved in the community. What social clubs do you belong to?" Such a question could elicit information about religious or other affiliations, establishing the basis for illegal discrimination.

## EXPERT TIP

**Pauline A. Javorski** has both a corporate and an academic perspective as HR director at the Coriell Institute for Medical Research, and also as an adjunct professor in the MBA leadership program at Holy Family University in Philadelphia. She describes seven types of job interviews:

- **Unstructured:** the interviewer has no plan other than "getting to know" the applicant. This approach feels less intimidating than more formal interviews, but affords little chance to compare the varied information provided by different candidates.

- **Behavioral Event Interview:** applicants are asked to relate past instances in which they have demonstrated specific job skills. This method is strongly favored in the HR community, because past behavior has been found to be the best predictor of future performance.

- **Panel or Committee:** conducted by a team, typically including a manager, an HR specialist, and one or more potential co-workers. Designed to observe communication skills in a group setting, this approach is popular in the science and academic communities.

- **Group Interview:** several applicants are simultaneously interviewed. This technique explores communication and leadership skills. Sometimes used in selecting college faculty, but not popular in business settings, because it seems too much like 'speed dating'—giving only a fleeting glimpse of each candidate.

- **Mealtime Interview:** when any of these interview techniques takes place over a meal. This usually happens as a follow-up, or when the selection process is nearly completed; lunch for mid-level, dinner for senior positions.

- **Audition:** for athletes, people in the performing arts, and others whose specific ability is of paramount importance, this type of interview is a demonstration session, with some questions asked during or afterward. One example in the business world involves temp office workers.

- **Stress:** trying to put the candidate off balance through a variety of "stressors," such as firing successive questions before the applicant completes answers to previous questions. Javorski is not a proponent of this approach, which promotes anxiety and is ineffective in gaining information on the applicant.

A list of questions HR experts generally advise interviewers to avoid is presented in Figure 16.2. However, given the numerous laws prohibiting discrimination, and since questions can be phrased in a variety of ways, no single list can be comprehensive. The best way to avoid problems that could lead to discriminatory behavior is to simply focus questions on the specific qualifications and ability to perform the tasks in the position.

More than 80 competencies have been defined for the great variety of occupations, and questions can be customized to focus on relevant knowledge, skills, and abilities. In Figure 16.3, we present a few examples that have common connections to many occupations, such as initiative, communication, and leadership.

---

**Figure 16.3**

### Behavioral Event Interview Questions

**Initiative**

- List two or three suggestions or new ideas you presented to your supervisor in the past 12 months. Were your ideas implemented?
- Name some problems you have tried to solve before being instructed to do so.
- Describe some situations in which a project was accomplished primarily due to your actions. What actions did you take?
- Give some examples of actions you took that were beyond what is normally expected from someone in your position. What were the results?

**Planning and Organization**

- How do you distinguish between what is urgent and what is not when setting priorities?
- What methods and tools do you use to schedule weekly activities for your section?
- Can you think of a period when your unit had a backlog of work? What caused the delays? What did you do?
- How far ahead do you schedule your time?

**Communication**

- Give me an example of an important written document you composed yourself.
- Do you give presentations or briefings very often?
- Describe a situation where you had to state your position strongly in order to get a point across.
- Can you think of a situation in which you didn't agree with a position someone was taking at a meeting, and you challenged them? Were you able to do it without ruffling feathers? How did you do it?

---

**Figure 16.3 continued**

**Leadership**

- Have you ever been in a situation in which you had to assert yourself as a team leader over a group of peers? How did you go about it?

- Can you describe actions you've taken over the past year to maintain trust and unity among employees?

- Can you describe how you have specifically modeled energy, enthusiasm, competence, commitment, and a hard-working attitude for others?

- Have you ever had an employee who had difficulty completing tasks? What action did you take to improve or deal with the issue?

**Motivation**

- Describe a situation in which you were able to have a positive influence on the action of others.

- Have you ever had a subordinate whose work was always marginal? How did you deal with that person?

**Resolving Conflict**

- Have you ever had to settle conflict between two people on the job? What was the situation and what did you do?

- Tell me about a time you were able to successfully deal with another person who may not have personally liked you.

## Questions to Identify Competencies

Let's imagine you've considered the different approaches, and want to ask something more focused than "Tell me about yourself?" The best approach is to conduct a Behavioral Event Interview. Here's how:

- Using a recently updated position description for the vacancy, identify key competencies—pick out the knowledge, skills, and abilities it takes to be effective in the job. It's helpful to bring others in on this, asking the opinions of fellow managers and any employees who might currently hold a position similar to the vacancy.

- For each competency, describe a job-related scenario in which knowledge, skill, or ability is demonstrated. Then ask applicants if they can describe a time when they experienced a similar situation. If so, ask them to provide details on decisions they made, actions they took, and the results (including any lessons they might have learned).

- Establish scoring criteria, especially if two or more interviewers will conduct the interviews. This can be as simple, for example, as giving five points for a detailed response, three points for an average response, and one point for a poor response. If time and inclination allow, you may wish to construct a more objective system, with greater quantification of elements in applicants' responses.

To create interview questions specific to your situation, you can find close examples—detailed behavioral interview questions, ready-to-use or easily adaptable—free on the Internet. Sites maintained by university HR departments and state offices of personnel are particularly thorough and useful (and they're not trying to sell you anything). Some good choices we've identified among these free sites are:

- Carnegie Mellon University: *http://www.cmu.edu/hr/recruit_staff/forms/ InterviewQuestionsBehavioral.pdf*

- Saginaw Valley State University: *http://www.svsu.edu/emplibrary/Focused%20 Questions%20by%20Compentency.pdf*

- Wisconsin School of Business: *http://ww.bus.wisc.edu/career/student/resumes/behavi oral/#behavioralinterviewoverview*

- North Carolina Office of State Personnel: *http://www.performancesolutions. nc.gov/staffinginitiatives/selection/docs/Selection_InterviewFormats_ BehaviorBasedInterviewQuestions.pdf*

## Showtime: Conduct the Interview and Follow Up

If you've prepared well for the interview, you can simply follow your agenda, ask the questions you've carefully prepared, and enjoy the show. But there are a few things to keep in mind:

- First, project a friendly but professional demeanor. Even if you're a person who normally engages in banter, this is not a time for humor. Applicants expect a serious tone, and if you engage in humor, it may unfairly put them off balance.

- As a comfortable conversation is established, don't slip up with those questions you should avoid (Figure 16.2). Keep in mind the prohibitions against discrimination and stay focused on specific elements of the job.

- Remember the importance of asking the same questions of all applicants, in as nearly the same way as possible.

- If you're using the behavioral interview approach, it's important to press for details when the applicant describes accomplishments.

- As applicants respond to questions, maintain an air of objectivity. Your comments should be neutral. Respond to their descriptions of experience by saying "thank you" and nodding your head, rather than comments like "very impressive" or "that's great."

- Beware of the "halo" effect, in which an applicant brings up something of particular interest to you, and too much time is spent discussing a single point. Stick to your agenda.

- Unless the applicant already works for your organization, take the opportunity at some point in the interview—probably toward the end, but it also could be earlier—to give a short "commercial" about the company. For example: it has a proud history, a good corporate culture, or is a good place to work.

- Keep notes about applicant responses, in order to compare with other applicants. Notes are also important in the event you need to defend against a subsequent complaint. If you've set up a scoring system, be sure to score all areas.

- Leave some time at the end of the interview for the applicant to ask questions, which you can prompt: "Do you have any questions for me?"

- Unless previously decided otherwise (by you and your superiors), remain noncommittal in your closing comments. An appropriate concluding statement is something like, "We appreciate your coming in to meet with us today. As you know, this selection process takes some time, and we'll be contacting you as soon as a decision is made."

# GIVE EMPLOYEE FEEDBACK

"The unexamined life is not worth living."

—*Socrates*

---

### In This Chapter

- General employee feedback.
- Specific guidance for employee feedback during performance reviews.
- How the manager prepares for it.
- How to recognize achievement.
- How to engage in straight talk on needed improvements.
- How to actively listen to the employee.
- How to handle disagreements.
- How to ensure key outcomes from the meeting.
- How to plan for follow-up.

---

It's performance appraisal time, a time most managers look forward to about as much as they would an annual medical checkup. Appraisals don't involve getting poked and prodded as much as physicals, but there are similarities. In both cases, most of the discussion will sound familiar. Physicians might be saying "could've eaten better and gotten more exercise;" managers might talk about "better prioritizing and accepting more responsibility." In both instances, there will be great relief when it's over—especially if there are no big surprises.

We can't tell you that giving employee feedback can be fun, any more than we can suggest you'll enjoy having your annual physical. But we can help you prepare and communicate job-performance feedback to your employees in a thoroughly professional manner.

First, there's a distinction between feedback and a performance appraisal or review. The terms range from general to specific. Giving feedback is the process of telling those who work for you what you think they're doing right, and where you think they need improvements. The performance appraisal or performance review is an event that takes place at a single point in time, when a manager provides a comprehensive evaluation of an employee's overall job performance. This assessment process normally consists of both a written report, often done on a form designed for the purpose, and a one-on-one discussion between the supervisor and the employee. The frequency of these two activities also distinguishes them: employee feedback can occur numerous times throughout the year, while the appraisal takes place at set intervals, usually once or twice a year.

One coaching concept that might be useful in the context of day-to-day employee feedback is termed the "10-60-90" adult learning principle (Minter and Thomas, 2000). It states that:

- If a manager tells the employee what to do, he will remember approximately **10 percent** of the job instructions.
- When the manager tells and shows the employee what to do, he will remember about **60 percent** of the information.
- When the manager tells and shows the employee what to do, and has the employee demonstrate what was observed, the employee will retain approximately **90 percent** of the instructions.

Giving feedback is constant. Performance reviews are more complex.

## The Setting: Employee/Manager Relations and Performance Appraisals

Employee/Manager relations—the overall realm of interaction between managers and employees—is a large and complex subject. For those with time and inclination to more deeply explore the subject of uniting the hearts and minds of employees and managers, we suggest these two in-depth resources:

- Jim Hauden's *The Art of Engagement: Bridging the Gap Between People and Possibilities*. Top-flight management consultant Hauden describes proven, effective ways to communicate, and to empower and motivate employees so everyone understands and feels inspired about their jobs.
- Paul Marciano's *Carrots and Sticks Don't Work: Build a Culture of Employee Engagement With the Principles of RESPECT*. Citing studies of human behavior, the Yale psychologist proposes that carrots and sticks be replaced by principles such as recognition, empowerment, partnering, and trust.

### Types of Performance-Appraisal Systems

The performance appraisal is administered as a formal process in most U.S. companies and nonprofit organizations. Steps involved in a successful appraisal process include

- setting performance objectives for each job

**EXPERT TIP**

"Nothing that happens in the formal, yearly review meeting should come as a shock to the employee, or to the manager," according to Jim Ellis, who served as president of Boat U.S., a boating membership organization with over half a million members. In Ellis' view, evaluations—and the employee feedback at the heart of it—should take place year-round. "You might only have a formal review meeting once a year, but a good manager does performance review every single day," he says. His suggestions on how to do that include:

- **Praise good work immediately**, whenever you see it.

- **Ask the employee how things are going, and listen**—sincerely and attentively —to the answers. "If I hear something that merits action, (something needs correcting or a good idea needs implementing), I'll act. But many times, people just want to be heard, to have the boss appreciate their frustrations, after which they proceed to resolve problems on their own."

- **Ask random questions** to make sure the employee is completely clear on assignments, tasks, and objectives.

- **Express curiosity about a work procedure**, so the employee will demonstrate what she is doing. Use this entrée to make sure nothing is confusing or distracting.

- **Monitor some work cycles to identify any difficult tasks**, and provide additional guidance if warranted.

- For tasks that continue to prove difficult, **discuss with the employee whether any training might be helpful** in improving the situation.

- establishing a rating system to measure the degree to which objectives were met
- recording actual performance
- discussing those elements between supervisor and employee
- creating a follow-up plan to target areas for improvement.

Several different approaches are briefly described below. They are not mutually exclusive; some parts of the techniques may be combined. For example, some essay writing may be included in the Trait/Behavior Checklist approach.

- **Trait/Behavior Checklist.** This most popular approach uses a checklist to rate employees in order to save time and minimize bias. The checklist contains specific performance criteria—typically 10–20 rating items tailored to the specific work situation. For each item, the employee can be rated by choosing a level of performance ranging from the high end (far exceeded expectations) to midrange (met expectations) to the low end (marginal performance or did not meet expectations). Various versions of this checklist approach provide three to seven possible rating choices.

- **Essay.** The form used to record information in this approach is simple. Supervisors provide substantial subjective commentary on the employee's performance. This is the most arduous method at rating time, because it is the least structured. Preparing the essay demands strong analytical and writing skills on the part of supervisors, and is usually reserved for reviewing the work of a small number of higher-level professional employees.

- **Critical Incident Technique.** In this approach, supervisors keep daily logs of what employees do, which is an inherently time-consuming process. And, it is often unpopular among employees because of the impression that the boss constantly keeps tabs on them.

- **Forced Ranking.** Employees are ranked relative to one another on a bell curve, which arbitrarily positions about 15 percent as high achievers, 70 percent as average, and 15 percent as marginal or poor performers. The premise is that companies must identify the best and worst workers; nurture the former, rehab or release the latter. We're not sure whether there's valid scientific evidence that actual performance reflects the forced distributions, but we are sure the approach leads to difficulty persuading employees the results are unbiased. Comments from HR professionals and in HR journals suggest that forced ranking results in the highest level of workforce dissatisfaction.

- **MBO (management by objective).** In this approach, specific objectives related to larger organizational goals are established, to be accomplished in a specified amount of time. There is no focus on traits or behavior, except as they relate to the achievement of goals. Analytical skills and good writing are needed to establish the objectives. Identifying specific goals that are realistic and achievable is always a challenge. Then, during review, if results are not clear-cut, supervisors must perform analyses to determine levels of progress, and often do a lot more writing. The time requirements and complexity of this approach normally limit its applicability to a few higher-level executives.

- **360-Degree Review.** This method is combined with one of the above approaches, but this review is performed not only by the supervisor and the employee, but also by the employee's peers, customers, and all others who come into contact with him in the work setting. The approach has obvious potential, but its popularity is limited because it is very time-consuming, with the need to explain and clarify instructions and then wait for responses from so many participants.

## Resources for Smaller Organizations

In medium-to-large organizations, one or more of the performance-review approaches are initiated and supported by the HR department. When appraisals are due, the requisite forms are furnished to managers, along with rating instructions and other guidance. Smaller organizations without HR departments have to develop and administer these systems for themselves, but web-based resources are readily available.

Many vendors sell off-the-shelf software that can deliver a comprehensive and customizable performance-appraisal system for up to 50 employees, for less than

$1,000 a year. These programs generate everything from the starting point form to establish performance standards for each employee, to the rating forms and guides for evaluating performance, to suggested language for use during the appraisal interview. Several choices can be found and compared by doing an Internet search for top-rated performance-appraisal software. Two of the top choices for small organizations are:

- ReviewSNAP by Applied Training Systems – *http://www.reviewsnap.com/*
- TrakStar Professional by Promantek – *http://www.promantek.com/*.

Customer reviews for both of these programs confirmed they were user-friendly, had responsive live support, and delivered thorough plans, forms, scoring instructions, and calendared reminders for managers.

Of course, small organizations can create their own performance-appraisal systems from scratch, cutting corners by copying procedures and forms found elsewhere. This is a fair amount of work, but the price is right. Several universities and other nonprofit organizations post example appraisal guides and forms on the Internet with no copyright restrictions.

Three excellent examples from university programs, which provide fairly complete instructions on how to use the forms, are listed below. The DePaul evaluation forms appear clean and simple, and they allow immediate comparison because they present self-assessment scores directly adjacent to the supervisor's scores. The FIU system uses four levels of rating. This forces the hand of supervisors a bit, away from the inclination to rate most employees in the middle, which often takes place when there are three or five levels of rating.

- DePaul University—*http://hr.depaul.edu/Performance/index.html*
- Florida International University—*http://hr.fiu.edu/uploads/file/forms/elr/usps_appraisal.pdf*
- Princeton University—*http://www.princeton.edu/hr/policies/conditions/5.1/5.1.3/perform_b.pdf*

Appraisal forms that can be copied free are available from some Internet sites that are sponsored by ads. One attractive resource is a site called "The Performance Appraisal Sharing Experience." It can be found online at: *http://www.whatmakesagoodleader.com/Performance-Appraisal.html*

## Project the Right Attitude About Performance Reviews

Now that we've seen what's involved in performance appraisals, it's time to think about that key conversation with the employee. The manager should be aware of how much is riding on an appraisal for the employee. The rating an employee receives may have implications for her livelihood and standing in the workplace, and it most certainly will have an impact on self-esteem. There is every reason for a manager to go into this process with the utmost professionalism: to be forthright but sympathetic, supportive but sincere.

In order to project those qualities during performance appraisals and to be credible, the manager must maintain a carefully measured attitude toward the review process. Clearly, a lot of negativity is associated with performance appraisals. We're not suggesting that managers become outspoken advocates, or even need to express fondness for the review process. But managers should have a basic understanding of the debate over the value of the performance appraisal, and a realistic appreciation of its use as a management tool.

To be credible in the process—whether the words are spoken out loud, given to employees in writing, or just remain an unspoken standpoint—managers should ascribe to the view that: "I know this performance review is an interruption from our regular schedule, and it's going to take up some of our time. Whether we like it or think it's a hassle, we have to accept that our organization uses this as a tool—to keep our work organized and make sure our objectives are clear. This review will give us the opportunity to recognize good performance, take note where we've missed the mark, and look for ways to improve. It's important for me to hear what you have to say about the job, and anything *you* think we might try to make things better. We also have the opportunity to talk about ways to improve your knowledge or skills—perhaps with some new training, or trying some different techniques. So let's work through this together, to improve the job and our team."

What kind of negative comments might you hear? In addition to routine grousing about wasting time, and ratings being just a "paperwork charade," you may occasionally hear a substantive challenge. A well-prepared detractor might even point out that some imposing business authorities hate performance reviews, including the legendary W. Charles Deming. The quality improvement guru did, in fact, say, "Fair ratings are impossible (1986)." He and others of like mind called the process too subjective and one-sided, and said it should be abolished.

The bottom line is, many more experts are on the other side of the debate, and they have prevailed, because 92 percent of U.S. companies engage in performance reviews. A convincing statement wrapping up the argument appeared in the *Harvard Business Review*, pointing out the problem is simply poor execution of a good idea: "Research has suggested that in two-thirds of cases, performance feedback elicits improved performance. Not only can reviews help employees recognize their strengths and developmental needs, but, if done well, can boost their motivation (Sytch and DeRue, 2010)."

## Plan and Conduct the Review Session

Now that you have context to the process—background, where to find forms, the proper mindset—it's time to suggest specific steps to complete the appraisal process. We'll show best practices to prepare materials, perform the rating, conduct the meeting with the employee, handle difficult circumstances, and follow through.

Now everything is in place, the performance review is due, and it's showtime. To quickly access bare essentials needed to determine the rating and to conduct the meeting, see Figure 17.1 "Determine the Rating," and Figure 17.2 "Conduct the Performance Review Meeting."

It's difficult to estimate the time needed to perform these tasks without knowing the type of positions involved, the particular type of performance-appraisal system in use, or the amount of background materials that must be reviewed. But we can make ballpark guesses, based on surveys across various occupations. The most popular review system is the Trait/Behavior Checklist, which takes less time than other systems—so we estimate analyzing the materials and determining the rating will take a minimum of two hours, and the review meeting will take one hour.

---

**Figure 17.1**

### Determine the Rating

- Start with an appraisal form, which will guide you through the review. If your organization doesn't have one, copy and modify a generic form from one of the sources listed in the chapter.
- Ask the employee to do a self-appraisal. Most systems provide a form for this, but if not, informally create one. A copy of your appraisal form will suffice. Ask for its completion and return before the appraisal interview.
- Gather the employee's job description, performance plan, last year's appraisal, and other documentation (such as records of training completed or classes attended).
- Retrieve any notes about day-to-day feedback with employee from your files.
- After reviewing the employee's performance plan, notes on actual performance and last year's review, and considering all other input, follow the sequence on the form to make decisions on individual rating areas. Be objective, candid, specific; evaluate performance, not personality; check the appropriate boxes on checklists; write essay text as called for on the form.  After reading over the individual section ratings, write an overall performance rating summary in the space provided.
- Sign the form and make two copies. Give one to the employee at the upcoming meeting; retain the other in the employee's personnel file.
- Arrange for meeting space to do the review; don't present your review across your desk. It's best to do this at a meeting table or in easy chairs, sitting next to the employee.
- Schedule the date and time (one hour is typically needed) with the employee. Clarify that the employee knows the purpose of the meeting, and has a chance to assemble any desired materials.

---

## The Value of Sample Phrases

In writing the text portions of performance appraisals, many busy managers find it helpful to refer to examples of language used in previously written reviews. Don't directly copy statements written about someone else in mindless cut-and-paste fashion. But there's nothing wrong with reviewing sample phrases on your work screen to jump-start word sequences, so you can then modify them into accurate statements about your subject employee. Here are links to two excellent sites on the Internet to find an abundance of effective sample phrases:

- "I Hate Performance Reviews." http://ihateperformancereviews.com/2010/06/communication-sample-performance-review-phrases/
- "Product-ivity: Your Guide to Brasher Business Decisions." http://product-ivity.com/performance-review-phrases/

---

**Figure 17.2**

### Conduct the Performance Review Meeting

- Maintain professional stature as a manager. It's OK to exhibit a friendly demeanor, but don't act like the employee's friend.
- Put the employee at ease.
- Set a positive, open tone—express positive expectations.
- Provide a preview of the interview:
  - We'll review the appraisal form; I'll explain my ratings and comments.
  - I'd like your opinion on the rating and on any job-related points you wish to make.
  - Then we'll set performance goals for the next rating period, and any completion dates.
  - Ask if the employee has any questions before getting to specifics.
- Give a copy of the appraisal form to the employee. Go over it point by point, explaining your comments. Remain objective, candid, specific; keep focused on performance, not personality.
- Ask the employee's opinion of the rating, or any other job-related subject. Listen actively and with an open mind; try to listen more (60 percent) than you talk (40 percent).
- If the employee is convincing on one or more points, say you will rethink the rating on those points, and will provide your decision in 24 hours. Reconsider carefully and inform the employee of your decision within the promised time period.
- Keep the discussion on track.
- Set specific performance expectations and goals for next rating period that are achievable, measurable, and realistic. Establish the timetable.
- Have the employee sign both copies of the appraisal form; the employee keeps one copy, and the other goes in the employee's personnel file.
- Thank the employee for participating in the process.

---

If you follow the step-by-step procedures for determining the rating (Fig. 17.1) and conducting the meeting with the employee (Fig. 17.2), you'll be successful. But you should also consider how to deal with employee reactions to the review. Nothing in the performance review should come as a shock to anyone in the meeting, but employees sometimes exhibit strong reactions upon receiving performance ratings.

Let's identify individuals you *don't* need to worry about in this discussion of dealing with difficult reactions. First are the high performers you rated as "far exceeded expectations" (they may express pleasure, or are quietly satisfied with their ratings). And second, a larger cohort of employees you rated as "met expectations," who generally agree with and accept their evaluation (quietly thinking of future improvement).

The folks to worry about are those displeased or distressed by their rating, and who are inclined either to resent it and challenge it, or to be depressed and despondent over it. See the expert tip for best practices on how to deal with these employees.

## Legal Considerations

Since performance appraisals are serious in nature—noting the impact they can have on self-esteem and livelihood—it doesn't take any stretch to imagine that legal troubles can result from sloppy or unfair reviews. To avoid legal difficulties, it's important the performance-appraisal process is conducted in a fair and objective manner, and also that proper documentation takes place along the way.

Some organizations enjoy HR staff support, which is fortunate. For those in smaller outfits or who go it alone, it is an extra challenge. HR professionals counsel from experience that there are nuances to the performance-appraisal process with significant legal implications. In addition to the need to be objective and to document as much as possible, the experts point to two areas of potential trouble:

1. In instances where management decides to terminate or demote an employee, past performance reviews should not contradict reasons stated for the adverse action. For example, if the reason cited for dismissing an employee was "Fred is difficult to work with," but the employee's recent performance appraisals contained the phrase "Fred is a good team player," the company would be in a weak position if the employee challenged the action in court. This is a strong reason to be candid in ratings; don't take the easy way out by sugarcoating bad behavior or inept performance. Be honest and specific in rating employees.

2. In routine performance appraisals, managers should avoid guaranteeing future employment, for example: "Sally showed great initiative again this period, and has a bright future with this company." Statements like that on a signed performance review can serve as an implied employment contract, with potential for future problems. This seems harsh, conveying that fear of lawsuits increasingly diminishes what managers can do or say; in this case, limiting positive comments about an employee. But there are many other ways to express satisfaction for work and praise for employees, so it shouldn't be difficult to avoid mentioning job longevity in reviews.

We can't offer guidance on how to avoid all legal risks in conducting and documenting performance reviews. When legal questions arise, or when in doubt about the legal implications of some aspect of the performance-review process, managers should seek advice from their HR professionals or general counsel. For those without in-house support, here's a reference specifically on this subject: *Dealing With Problem Employees: a Legal Guide*, written by lawyer Amy DelPo (2011).

**EXPERT TIP**

**Dick Grote**, a noted authority on performance evaluation (2010), tells how to deal with extreme employee reaction when receiving appraisals, which he describes as the "fight-or-flight response." Employees on the "fight" side of the equation typically exhibit anger, and are likely to deny the accuracy of information in the rating, or to blame others. On the "flight" side of the response, employees are likely to react with silence, and not only agree with the rating, but may inwardly accept more responsibility for a problem than is actually warranted. Grote suggests how to deal with either situation.

First, with the employee who exhibits defensive or angry behavior:

- **Remain calm**; maintain your own temper. (As the angry person speaks louder, modulate your own voice to be progressively softer. It may cool things down.)

- **Try to maintain eye contact to show sincerity**.

- **Seek to defuse any atmosphere of hostility** with a reminder like: "We are all members of a team, and while we have disagreements, everyone is important to the team."

- **Let the employee get out everything he has to say**.

- **Actively listen and restate to confirm what you've heard**, and to ensure you understand.

- **Focus the discussion on performance standards**; do not get into personalities or relationships.

- **Don't try to resolve all disagreements at the meeting**; instead, note points of disagreement and, if appropriate, promise future efforts to resolve problems and conflicts.

- **Be firm about the bottom-line requirements** decided as a result of your review.

- While not making any promises for the future, **clearly state what's required to get to a satisfactory job performance**.

Second, with the person who exhibits silence and withdrawal:

- **Be patient and friendly**.

- **Explain to the employee that you want his opinion** and that it's important to you.

- **Express concern about the employee**; mention they're being unresponsive and ask for their comments.

- **After the above step, maintain silence yourself**, even for a longish period of time—waiting for the employee to speak.

- **Ask open-ended questions**, and press them to expound on monosyllabic answers.

- **Ask the employee to recap** what you're asking them to do.

# EPILOGUE

In 1912, 100 years before this book, President Theodore Roosevelt gave a speech at the University of Paris. He said:

*"It is not the critic who counts; nor the man who points out how the strong man stumbles, or where the doer of deeds could have done them better. The credit belongs to the man who is actually in the arena, whose face is marred by dust and sweat and blood; who strives valiantly; who errs, who comes short again and again, because there is no effort without error and shortcoming; but who does actually strive to do the deeds; who knows great enthusiasms, the great devotions; who spends himself in a worthy cause; who at the best knows in the end the triumph of high achievement, and who at the worst, if he fails, at least fails while daring greatly, so that his place shall never be with those cold and timid souls who neither know victory nor defeat."*

Managers fight in the arena every day. They do great deeds and small ones; they succeed and fail; they make mistakes and fight on. With these tools, you can communicate better with your staff, peers, leaders, and the public. We salute you for assuming the challenges of management; to not only work hard yourself, but also to motivate others to do their best work. President Roosevelt also said, "Far and away the best prize life offers is the opportunity to work hard at work worth doing." Managing others is work that's very much worth doing.

If you'd like more help, check our website *www.managerscommunicationtoolbox.com*, where you'll find additional tricks and suggestions to help continue your development as a communicator. On our website, you'll find news about training programs we're conducting based on information in this book. We hope you'll get the opportunity to attend one of those sessions. You can also provide feedback on the site. We would like to hear from you if you agree or disagree with us, or if you have examples to tell us about.

We wish you success in your career. Thanks for reading!

Everett A. Chasen

Robert R. Putnam

October 2012

# ACKNOWLEDGMENTS

No book can be completed without help. We thank all those who gave generously of their time to help us put together the information we've provided for you. They include Justice Efrain L. Alvarado; Robert M. Baugh; James F. Ellis; Amy Myers Goldstein; Mary R. Grealy; Arthur S. Hamerschlag; Tom Harvey; Barbara Jacksier; Pauline A. Javorski; Dr. Robert Kole; Dr. Michael J. Kussman; Stewart Liff; Dr. Dana Moore; Katrice Pasteur; Ronald K. Peterson; the Hon. Anthony J. Principi; Joanne Richter; Laurence A. Silverman; Terry Gerigk Wolf; Claire L. Wudowsky; and Kimberly Zeich.

Don Smith, editor extraordinaire, contributed many valuable suggestions to the text that significantly improved our work. Our editor at ASTD, Heidi Smith, did a remarkable job of helping us shape the final form the book has taken. She has our admiration, our respect, and our deepest gratitude. We are also grateful to the Fairfax County, Virginia Public Library system and their wonderful research librarians for their assistance, and to Kristin Husak for recognizing the potential in our idea.

We thank our families for giving us the love, support, and time we needed to research and write this book. Finally, we thank all of the supervisors we have had in our careers, both good and bad. Their influence, and the many things we've learned from them, can be found on every page.

# REFERENCES

Adler, M., and C. Van Doren. (1972). *How to Read a Book: the Classic Guide to Intelligent Reading.* New York: Simon & Schuster.

Alessandra, T., and P. Hunsaker. (1993). *Communicating at Work.* New York: Simon & Schuster.

Birren, F. (1961). *Color Psychology and Color Therapy: A Factual Study of the Influence of Color on Human Life.* New York: Kessinger Publishing.

Byrne, J.A. (2005). "The Fast Company Interview: Jeff Immelt." *Fast Company.* http://www.fastcompany.com/magazine/96/jeff-immelt.html.

Cava, R. (2006). *Dealing With Difficult People.* Buffalo, NY: Firefly Books.

Covert, J., and T. Sattersten. (2009). *The 100 Best Business Books of All Time.* New York: The Penguin Group.

DelPo, A. (2011). *Dealing With Problem Employees: A Legal Guide, 6th edition.* Berkeley, CA: Nolo Publishing.

Deming, W.C. (1986). *Out of the Crisis, 2nd edition.* Cambridge, MA: MIT Press.

de Tocqueville, A. (1835). *De la democratie en Amerique (Democracy in America).* New York: Signet Classics.

Flora, C. (2004). "The Once-Over." *Psychology Today* 37: 60-64.

Gabarro, J.J., and J.P. Kotter. (2008). *Managing Your Boss.* Boston: Harvard Business School Press.

GE. (2007). "Letter to Investors." www.ge.com/ar2007/ltr_highperf.jsp.

Grote, D. (2010). "Overcoming Defensiveness in Employee Performance Evaluation Discussions." Articles3K.com. http://www.articles3k.com/article/426/151943/ Overcoming_Defensiveness_in_Employee_Performance_Evaluation_Discussions/

Hargie, O., D. Dixon, and D. Tourish. (1998). *Communication in Management.* Brookfield, VT: Gower Publishing House.

Hauden, J. (2008). *The Art of Engagement: Bridging the Gap Between People and Possibilities.* New York: McGraw-Hill.

Hyatt, M. (2007). "Finding More 'Head Time.'" *http://michaelhyatt.com/finding-more-"head-time".html.*

Kinsey Goman, C. (2011). "Seven Seconds to Make a First Impression." *Forbes Magazine.* http://www.forbes.com/sites/carolkinseygoman/2011/02/13/seven-seconds-to-make-a-first-impression/

Marciano, P. (2010). *Carrots and Sticks Don't Work: Build a Culture of Employee Engagement With the Principles of RESPECT.* New York: McGraw-Hill.

Mayer, R.E., and R. Moreno. (2005). *A Cognitive Theory of Multimedia Learning: Implications for Design Principles.* New York: Cambridge University Press.

Mehrabian, A., and M. Wiener. (1967). "Decoding of Inconsistent Communications." *Journal of Personality and Social Psychology* 6(1): 109–114. doi:10.1037/h0024532.

Meyer, H.E. (2010). *How to Analyze Information: A Step-By-Step Guide to Life's Most Vital Skill.* New York: Storm King Press.

Minter, R.L., and E.G.Thomas. (2000). "Employee Development Through Coaching, Mentoring, and Counseling: A Multidimensional Approach." *Review of Business* 21 (1/2): 43-47.

Morgan, N. (2009). *Public Words Blog.* http://publicwords.typepad.com/nickmorgan/2009/05/humor-in-public-speaking-1-how-to-use-traditional-humor.html.

Morkes, J., and J. Nielsen. (1997). "How to Write for the Web." http:/www.useit.com/papers/webrwriting/writing.html.

Noah, T. (1999). "For the Record, What Off the Record Means." *Slate Magazine.* http://www.slate.com/id/1003063/

Orwell, G. (1946). "Politics and the English Language." *Horizon Magazine.* London, UK.

Shipley, D., and W. Schwalbe. (2007). *Send: the Essential Guide to Email for Office and Home.* New York: Alfred A. Knopf.

Song, M., V. Halsey, and T. Burress. (2007). *The Hamster Revolution.* San Francisco: Berrett-Koehler Publishers.

Stark, P.B. (2011). "Employees and Decision Making." www.peterstark.com/employees-decision-making.

Swenson, R. (1992). *Margin: Restoring Emotional, Physical, Financial, and Time Reserves to Overloaded Lives*. Colorado Springs, CO: NavPress.

Sytch, M., and D. S. DeRue. (2010). "Ditch Performance Reviews? How About Learn to Do Them Well?" *Harvard Business Review*. http://blogs.hbr.org/cs/2010/06/ditch_performance_reviews_how.html.

The Management Standards Consultancy. "Evaluate Options." http://www.beabettermanager.com/dispchecklist.asp?pid=KA1S2C5

The National Commission on Writing for America's Families, Schools, and Colleges. (2004). *Writing: a Ticket to Work…or a Ticket Out: a Survey of Business Leaders*. New York: College Board Press.

The Pew Research Center. (2009). "The Pew Research Center's Internet & American Life Project: Parent-Teen Cell Phone Survey."

Richard, O.C. (2000). "Racial Diversity, Business Strategy, and Firm Performance: a Resource-Based View." *Academy of Management Journal* 43(2).

# ABOUT THE AUTHORS

**Everett A. (Ev) Chasen** is a partner in Foxwood Communications LLC, a communication consulting firm offering writing, mentoring, and communications planning services to companies and government agencies in the Washington, D.C. area. Ev is a former member of the Federal Senior Executive Service and was Chief Communications Officer for the Veterans Health Administration, the nation's largest healthcare organization. In this position, he had overall responsibility for the Administration's public relations, congressional affairs, voluntary service, web communication, and executive correspondence programs.

During his 35-year career with the U.S. government, Ev was a speechwriter for two cabinet secretaries, the senior news media spokesperson for the Department of Veterans Affairs (VA), the Department's Chief of Protocol, and held a number of other significant public affairs and administrative positions with VA and the U.S. Army Corps of Engineers. He has also been a freelance writer, a communications trainer, and an editor and writer for a number of employee publications.

**Robert R. (Bob) Putnam** has provided public relations counsel to (and written speeches for) top officials at several well-known national healthcare associations, as well as for a Congressional Commission and a U.S. Senator. During different administrations spanning 20 years, Bob was senior speechwriter for successive leaders of the U.S. Department of Veterans Affairs, serving members of the president's cabinet from both political parties.

Bob has been a communications trainer, has edited three books— including the *History of VA Medical Research*, by Marguerite T. Hayes, MD—and has served as national communications chairman of the society of federal medical agencies. Early in his career, working as a newspaper reporter, he won the Maryland-Delaware-D.C. Press Association's top honors for feature writing.

# INDEX

# Z